REMEMBER THE ALAMO

REMEMBER THE ALAMO

Everything You've Ever Wanted to Know About American History with All the Boring Bits Taken Out

ALISON RATTLE and ALLISON VALE

DELACORTE PRESS

Published in the United States by Delacorte Press,
an imprint of The Random House Publishing Group,
a division of Random House, Inc., New York.

DELACORTE PRESS is a registered trademark of Random House, Inc.,
and the colophon is a trademark of Random House, Inc.

Originally published in Great Britain by
Michael O'Mara Books Limited in 2009.

ISBN 978-0-385-34381-7

Printed in the United States of America

Book design by www.glensaville.com

A Book Club Edition

CONTENTS

The Birth of the United States

American Expansion and Reform

The Civil War

Reconstruction and Industrialization

TIME LINE

REVOLUTIONARY AMERICA

1763	King George's Proclamation Line
1764–67	Britain imposes a series of unpopular taxes
1770	The Boston Massacre
1773	The Boston Tea Party
1774	Britain imposes the Intolerable Acts
	The First Continental Congress is convened
1775–81	The Revolutionary War
1775	Paul Revere's "Midnight Ride"
	The Second Continental Congress is convened
1776	Betsy Ross sews the first American flag
	Signing of the Declaration of Independence
	Washington crosses the Delaware
1778	France recognizes the "United States of America"
1781	Signing of the Articles of Confederation

THE BIRTH OF THE UNITED STATES

1783	Britain officially relinquishes all claims to the United States in the Treaty of Paris
1786	Shays' Rebellion
1787	The Constitutional Convention is convened
1789	Signing of the United States Constitution
	George Washington becomes the first president of the United States
1790	Washington, DC is established as the capital city
1791	Signing of the Bill of Rights
1792	Formation of the first Republican (or Democratic-Republican) Party
1793	Eli Whitney invents the cotton gin
1798–1800	The Quasi-War between the United States and France

THE CIVIL WAR

RECONSTRUCTION AND INDUSTRIALIZATION

WORLD WAR ONE AND THE ROARING TWENTIES

1914–18	World War One
1915	The sinking of the *Lusitania*
1917	Interception of the "Zimmermann Telegram"
	The United States enters the war
1918	Wilson's Fourteen Points
1919	The Treaty of Versailles
	The Eighteenth Amendment introduces Prohibition
	The Nineteenth Amendment grants women the right to vote
1923	Commercial "talkies" are pioneered in New York City
1926	*Don Juan* is the first feature-length film with synchronized sound
1929	St. Valentine's Day Massacre takes place in Chicago

THE GREAT DEPRESSION AND WORLD WAR TWO

1929	The Wall Street Crash
1930s	The Great Depression
	The Dust Bowl
1931	"The Star-Spangled Banner" is officially adopted as the national anthem
1932	Franklin D. Roosevelt's "New Deal"
1933	The Twenty-First Amendment repeals Prohibition
1935–39	Congress passes four Neutrality Acts
1939–45	World War Two
1941	Japanese attack on Pearl Harbor
	The United States enters the war
1944	D-Day
1945	Atomic bomb attacks on Hiroshima and Nagasaki

POSTWAR AMERICA AND THE VIETNAM WAR YEARS

1945	The United Nations is founded
1945–90	Era of the Cold War
1947	The Marshall Plan
1948	The US Army is desegregated
1948–49	The Berlin Airlift
1950–53	The Korean War
1950–54	The McCarthy Witch Hunts
1954	*Brown v. Board of Education*
1955	The first American troops are sent to Vietnam
	The Montgomery Bus Boycott
1956	Public transportation is desegregated
1957	The Eisenhower Doctrine
1961	The Bay of Pigs invasion
1962	The Cuban Missile Crisis
1963	Martin Luther King, Jr.'s "I have a dream" speech
	Assassination of President John F. Kennedy
1964	The Gulf of Tonkin Resolution
	The Civil Rights Act
1965	The Voting Rights Act
	Establishment of the Medicare and Medicaid programs
	Assassination of Malcolm X
1965–73	The Vietnam War
1966	The Black Panthers are founded
1968	Assassination of Martin Luther King, Jr.
1969	Neil Armstrong becomes the first man on the moon
1969–70	Nixon's "secret war" in Cambodia
1972	Break-in at the Watergate complex
1973	*Roe v. Wade*
1974	The House of Representatives begins impeachment proceedings against Nixon
	President Nixon resigns

LIST OF PRESIDENTS OF THE UNITED STATES

	Name	Years in office
1	George Washington	1789–97
2	John Adams	1797–1801
3	Thomas Jefferson	1801–09
4	James Madison	1809–17
5	James Monroe	1817–25
6	John Quincy Adams	1825–29
7	Andrew Jackson	1829–37
8	Martin Van Buren	1837–41
9	William Henry Harrison	1841
10	John Tyler	1841–45
11	James K. Polk	1845–49
12	Zachary Taylor	1849–50
13	Millard Fillmore	1850–53
14	Franklin Pierce	1853–57
15	James Buchanan	1857–61
16	Abraham Lincoln	1861–65
17	Andrew Johnson	1865–69
18	Ulysses S. Grant	1869–77
19	Rutherford B. Hayes	1877–81
20	James A. Garfield	1881
21	Chester A. Arthur	1881–85
22	Grover Cleveland	1885–89
23	Benjamin Harrison	1889–93
24	Grover Cleveland	1893–97
25	William McKinley	1897–1901
26	Theodore Roosevelt	1901–09
27	William H. Taft	1909–13
28	Woodrow Wilson	1913–21
29	Warren G. Harding	1921–23
30	Calvin Coolidge	1923–29

31	Herbert C. Hoover	1929–33
32	Franklin D. Roosevelt	1933–45
33	Harry S. Truman	1945–53
34	Dwight D. Eisenhower	1953–61
35	John F. Kennedy	1961–63
36	Lyndon B. Johnson	1963–69
37	Richard Nixon	1969–74
38	Gerald Ford	1974–77
39	Jimmy Carter	1977–81
40	Ronald Reagan	1981–89
41	George H.W. Bush	1989–93
42	Bill Clinton	1993–2001
43	George W. Bush	2001–09
44	Barack Obama	2009–

COLONIAL AMERICA

COLUMBUS AND OTHER DISCOVERERS OF AMERICA
1492 and earlier

When Christopher Columbus encountered the "New World" in 1492, it was already home to an estimated 40–80 million people. The first Americans had splintered into tribes spanning the continents: from the Inuit in the north to the Yaghan of the Tierra del Fuego.

Until recently it was held that, when the Bering Land Bridge disappeared, American tribes were cut off from the rest of the world until Columbus's arrival. This neat history is now widely contested, undermined by discoveries such as that of an eleventh-century Viking settlement led by Leif Eriksson in what the fifteenth-century Italian adventurer John Cabot named "New Found Land." There are also claims that both Ireland's Saint Brendan and a Welsh prince called Madoc discovered America, while more convincing theories involve seafaring West Africans making it across the Atlantic.

Although Columbus, an Italian, was certainly not the first European on American soil, his seamanship and fearless determination were nonetheless remarkable. Funded by Queen Isabella of Spain, Columbus and his crew set sail aboard the *Niña*, the *Pinta* and the *Santa Maria* in search of a faster trade route from Europe to the spice riches of Asia, traveling west rather than east. Instead, he landed in the Bahamas, mistakenly referring to its inhabitants as "Indios" since he thought he was in East Asia.

Columbus is credited with advancing a general European awareness of the American continents; the anniversary of his voyage is observed on October 12 in Spain and on the second Monday of October in the United States.

THE CONQUISTADORS AND THE RISING CREOLE POPULATION
1500s

News of Columbus's New World quickly spread across Europe, inspiring many to follow his lead, including another Italian, Amerigo Vespucci, whose forename gave the Americas their name. The Spanish crown backed the Conquistadors—adventurers hardened to conflict as a way of life—led variously by Hernán Cortés and Francisco Pizarro. Pursuing personal glory, the Conquistadors colonized and subjugated the New World. Vast numbers of Native Americans were annihilated through violence, overwork, and European diseases to which they had no resistance.

By 1550, Conquistadors had claimed most of South and Central America, as well as Cuba, Mexico, and Florida. At first, Florida was simply a naval base, protecting the valuable Spanish treasure fleet from rampant piracy. But when, in 1562, a small colony of French Protestants settled there, the Spanish crown ordered their massacre and made Florida the first Spanish colony in America.

Throughout the seventeenth century, Spain's influence slackened as recession and the Thirty Years' War in Europe drained its resources. Culturally liberated, Spanish America developed its own "Creole" identity and the population exploded. During the eighteenth century, new Spanish settlements were established in California, Arizona, New Mexico, and Texas.

Spanish ascendancy was eventually curbed by the British, who took control of Florida in 1763. At the same time, the Creoles, inspired by revolutionary politics, clamored for independence. The days of Spain's American Empire were numbered.

THE ENGLISH QUEST FOR COLONIES AND A NORTHWEST PASSAGE
1558–1609

When the Protestant Queen Elizabeth I came to the English throne in 1558, the fiercely Catholic King Philip II of Spain, grown wealthy from his New World colonies, saw England as his biggest threat. Elizabeth, ambitious for an empire, fanned the flames, sponsoring piracy against the Spanish treasure fleet.

The English also wanted to defeat Spain in the search for a faster trade route to India and China. Convinced that a Northwest Passage could be found by sailing up the coast of the New World and through the Arctic, several French and English explorers tried and failed. Later, in 1609, the Dutch hired Englishman Henry Hudson to try. Hudson gave his name to the bay and the river, and the area provided the English with a lucrative trade in fur, but he never found the elusive passage, and later disappeared when his crew mutinied following a grueling Arctic winter.

In 1585, Elizabeth gave her blessing to an English expedition to claim colonies in the New World, from which it was hoped Spanish treasure ships might be intercepted and raided. Sir Walter Raleigh— and Sir Francis Drake a year later—founded a very small English colony on Roanoke Island on North Carolina's Outer Banks. But English supply ships, preoccupied with the Spanish Armada in 1588 and further delayed by bad weather and piracy, were unable to return to America until 1590, by which time the colonists had mysteriously vanished.

The Lost Colony was Queen Elizabeth I's last American venture, although Virginia was named after her (the "Virgin Queen") by Raleigh.

JAMESTOWN: THE FIRST ENGLISH SETTLEMENT IN AMERICA
1607

By the end of Elizabeth I's reign, adventurers were far more attracted to plundering Spanish treasure than to costly colonization. But in 1605, during the reign of James I, two wealthy English merchant groups merged to form the Virginia Company, and provided the vast capital needed to establish an American colony.

In 1607, 500 English colonists landed at Chesapeake Bay and built Jamestown. A malarial swamp and undrinkable river water made the site a bad choice, and drought, famine, and disease all but exterminated the colony and drove some to cannibalism. By 1610, only sixty survived.

Colonist John Smith soon took leadership. According to legend, Smith's life was saved in 1608 by eleven-year-old Pocahontas, daughter of the chief of the Powhatan. Smith quickly earned the trust of Chief Powhatan—whose assistance initially kept the colonists alive—but hostilities returned when local tribes felt threatened by the colonists' expansion, and continued long after Smith left to found New England in 1609. A temporary peace was achieved when settler John Rolfe married Pocahontas in 1614.

Rolfe transformed Jamestown's fortunes with a new, exportable strain of tobacco, and the colony grew. Meanwhile, the Virginia Company was making gradual improvements in colonists' rights in an attempt to draw more people to the settlement. In 1619, Jamestown's House of Burgesses—a sort of parliament—became the first elected governing body in Virginia, and indeed in the New World. It was North America's first step toward democratic government.

PURITANS AND PILGRIMS
1560s–1620

The sixteenth-century English Reformation saw the English Church break away from Roman Catholicism to create a new Protestant Church of England. But a minority of Protestants felt that the English Church had not done enough to rid itself of what they considered to be lavish Catholic superstitions. This minority became known as Puritans, because they wanted to "purify" the English Church.

By the end of Elizabeth I's reign, a growing number of Puritans wanted to separate from the Church of England, which they regarded as ungodly and corrupt. Some Separatist Puritans eventually did sever relations, establishing an independent hierarchy of congregations and "elders" that was generally regarded with great suspicion. In 1608, with religious intolerance in England reaching its peak, the Separatists fled to Holland to escape persecution.

By 1618, this same congregation—frustrated by financial insecurity and the difficulties of raising a younger generation amid the many "extravagant" temptations of Holland—had determined to make a fresh start on English-owned soil, near the Virginia colony. They now saw themselves as "pilgrims" and their emigration as an opportunity to take their religious convictions to a place unfettered by corrupt European Christianity.

The Pilgrims' application for permission to settle within English territories in America encountered numerous obstacles but was eventually approved. In September 1620, they set sail from Plymouth aboard the *Mayflower*.

THE *MAYFLOWER* AND PLYMOUTH ROCK
1620

The Pilgrims on board the *Mayflower* steered a course for the mouth of the Hudson River, at the northern tip of the Virginia colony. But rough seas pushed the ship hundreds of miles off course, forcing a landing outside of English territory, at Cape Cod Bay.

Fifty non-Puritan passengers seized this opportunity to declare themselves exempt from English rule. The Pilgrim leaders, motivated to emigrate so that they might correct what they saw as an ungodly society, could not allow disorder at this early stage. They drew up the Mayflower Compact—laws with which almost all the men on board agreed to abide—and elected John Carver as the colony's first governor. This was the first written constitution in North America.

The *Mayflower* Pilgrims left Cape Cod and sailed on to Plymouth Rock, a place previously named and mapped by Captain John Smith. Mirroring the early trials of the Jamestown settlers, the Pilgrims' first few months were marked by hardship; 50 of the 102 colonists died during the harsh winter, including John Carver, who was succeeded by William Bradford.

But, just as at Jamestown, the settlers' survival was secured by the support of the Native Americans, in this case the Wampanoag, whose chief, Massasoit, marked the Pilgrims' first harvest with a three-day feast of turkey, venison, pumpkin, and corn, one of the earliest recorded Thanksgiving celebrations. Hard work and trade with Native Americans helped the colony prosper and inspired the "Great Migration" of Puritans to America.

SLAVERY AND THE
FIRST PLANTATIONS
1611–19

Jamestown settler John Rolfe produced his first harvest of Virginian tobacco in 1611, kick-starting a long and profitable European obsession with the American crop. By 1624, tobacco planters were the new Virginian aristocracy, growing 200,000 pounds of it every year. By the 1680s, this had soared to a staggering 3 million pounds. This inevitably led to a scramble for labor, and thousands of indentured English servants crossed the Atlantic to face the notoriously harsh conditions on the plantations. They had few rights, but were generally guaranteed their freedom after five years' service.

Demand for labor soon outstripped supply, however, and Chesapeake planters duly turned to the increasingly prolific "traffic in men" from West Africa. (In 1619, when the first cargo of African slaves arrived in Jamestown, there were already more than a million of them in South America.) Until the end of the seventeenth century, the slave trade was slower in the North, whose workforce was made up of English servants working alongside African slaves. But as Virginia's African population grew, so too did the legal distinction between the two workforces, and slaves' rights diminished.

By the end of the eighteenth century, over 2 million African slaves had been brought to the colonies and made up around 50 percent of the population. White supremacy had become firmly entrenched in law, and slavery entirely underpinned the economy.

THE RUSH FOR
RELIGIOUS FREEDOM
1629–82

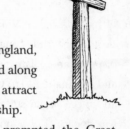

With religious intolerance rampant in England, many new English colonies were settled along the Atlantic seaboard, where they continued to attract religious communities seeking freedom of worship.

The success of the first Puritan settlers prompted the Great Migration of 1629–42, when thousands of English Puritans decamped to Massachusetts, founding Salem and Boston. Meanwhile, in 1634, 200 settlers founded Maryland, a spiritually tolerant colony that welcomed Catholics and was named for Henrietta Maria, King Charles I's Catholic wife.

Roger Williams, whose controversial views saw him driven into the wilderness by both England and Puritan Massachusetts, founded the nonconformist haven of Providence, Rhode Island, in 1636, on land sold to him by the Narragansett Indians. Williams preached that church and state should be entirely separate and advocated absolute freedom of worship. More scandalous still, he believed that no royal charter could justify taking Native Americans' land by force.

By the time Quakers (established in 1648) began arriving, Rhode Island was the only New England colony without anti-Quaker laws. In 1682, fervent Quaker William Penn founded Pennsylvania ("Penn's Woods"). He respected the rights of Native Americans and agreed to take control only of land he could comfortably walk in three days. Pennsylvania became a vibrant, pacifist colony, and Penn's legacy was an enlightened attitude toward both democracy and equality, while embracing traditional Quaker ideals such as modesty of clothing and language.

THE SALEM WITCH TRIALS
1692–93

In 1689, Salem Village (now Danvers), Massachusetts, established its first Puritan congregation under minister Samuel Parris. Factional disputes about Parris's appointment soon arose, fomenting mistrust and speculation as to God's will in the matter. When Parris's daughter and niece began suffering inexplicable fits in 1692, the atmosphere was ripe for cries of possession by the Devil. As the villagers sought to discover who had "afflicted" the girls, reports of witchcraft spread, and new afflictions were reported in Salem and beyond.

When pressed to identify their tormentors, the victims named two local outcasts and one slave, who were promptly interrogated and imprisoned. By early summer, dozens of women and men were in custody; while some had confessed to witchcraft, others had merely voiced uncertainty at the surreal proceedings.

At the end of May, Sir William Phips, Governor of Massachusetts, ordered that the accused be tried in a court of Oyer and Terminer (from French: "hear and determine"). The trials ran for a year, with most indictments based on "spectral evidence"—the testimonies of the afflicted—and were only halted when cases became particularly unconvincing. By this time, nineteen people had been hanged and numerous others had died in prison. Contrary to popular myth, none was burned at the stake.

Scientists now believe that rye infected with ergot—a fungus that can produce hallucinations—caused the affliction. In 1706, victim Ann Putnam apologized for her part in the deaths of people "whom now I have just grounds and good reason to believe they were innocent persons; and that it was a great delusion of Satan that deceived me in that sad time."

FRENCH AMERICA
1608–1763

In 1608, a fur-trading company sponsored Frenchman Samuel de Champlain to embark upon a North American exploration. He founded the colony of Quebec, befriended the Huron and Algonquin tribes, and began trading with them for furs. The French trade in North American furs grew into a lucrative business.

French interest in the colony remained trade-focused, with the monarchy reluctant to sponsor large-scale migration; rumors that Canada was an icebound, savage land did much to stem what enthusiasm there may have been for emigration. By 1700, "New France" was populated by only 19,000 Frenchmen; less than 20 percent of its European population was made up of women, and most of them were nuns.

The French monarchy did, however, sponsor the Company of New France, which largely monopolized trade in the colony, and, from the 1640s onward, encouraged the gradual expansion of its borders. A succession of adventurers and missionaries steadily extended the boundaries of New France southward along the Mississippi. By 1671, the French had claimed a vast section of western North America that stretched from Quebec to the Gulf of Mexico, which they named Louisiana, in honor of King Louis XIV.

With an economy reliant upon the fur trade rather than on land-grabbing agriculture, relations between the French and the local Native Americans were largely good; so good, in fact, that French officials complained about Frenchmen being attracted into the Native American lifestyle. But when the French colonists helped the tribes of the Huron Confederacy defeat the Iroquois, the powerful Huron became the colony's greatest threat.

NEW NETHERLAND: DUTCH AMERICA
1609–64

The Dutch dominated seventeenth-century commerce and boasted the world's largest merchant navy. Having staked a claim to the Hudson Bay area in 1609, the Dutch, like the French, regarded North America as an opportunity to profit from trade rather than territory. They established a small trading outpost in what is now Albany, New York, and began a fur trade.

By 1624, there were two Dutch settlements in the New Netherland region. One was New Amsterdam, a trading village at the mouth of the Hudson; the other was Manhattan Island, which the Dutch famously bought from local Native Americans for $24. This respectful relationship wasn't always typical: Territorial disputes caused a three-year war with the Algonquin in the 1640s, while the murder of a Dutch farmer in 1643 led the Dutch to decapitate eighty members of the Wappinger tribe as they slept.

The Dutch left their mark on New Amsterdam, whose more relaxed moral code attracted a very different kind of settler than Puritan New England. By the 1630s, with more taverns in existence than churches, there were already eighteen distinct languages to be heard. The smaller settlements of Breuckelen (Brooklyn) and Nieuw Haarlem (Harlem) sprung up nearby, while a defensive wall marking New Amsterdam's northern boundary gave the future Wall Street its name.

But the balance of power in New Amsterdam remained firmly with wealthy landowners, making for an undemocratic, unregulated system. In 1664, when English troopships arrived in New Amsterdam harbor, the settlers readily acquiesced and New Amsterdam became New York (after James, Duke of York, brother of King Charles II).

THE INDIAN WARS OF THE SEVENTEENTH CENTURY
1637 onward

Although many Native American tribes had offered America's colonists invaluable help, colonial expansion inevitably led to an increasing mistrust between the two populations. In the early seventeenth century, New England's Puritans began subduing what they saw as a Native American threat to their way of life.

The first battle came in 1637, when Boston preachers encouraged a war against the Pequot, a Mohican clan. Taking them by surprise at night, the Puritans burned dozens of villages and decimated a town of 600 inhabitants, annihilating almost the entire clan.

In southern New England in 1675, a change in Puritan policy toward former allies the Wampanoag prompted Chief Metacom—nicknamed King Philip because of his penchant for European attire—to declare war. The Wampanoag were well equipped and formed an alliance with other local tribes, and "King Philip's War" became one of the most vicious ever fought on American soil. By 1676, over half of New England's ninety towns had come under attack. The Puritans enlisted the aid of local Mohicans and overwhelmed the Wampanoag, decapitating Metacom and selling his wife and son into slavery.

Beyond New England, other tribes were suffering similar fates, escalated by the Dutch policy of scalp taking. By 1722, with scalps fetching a staggering 100 pounds sterling apiece (around $4,000 in today's money), the image of the Native American as a savage was firmly etched into the New England consciousness.

THE FRENCH AND INDIAN WAR
1754–63

From the end of the seventeenth century, European imperial rivalries prompted a series of wars on American soil. By 1748, Spain had lost its claim to North America, and France and Britain were left to face the biggest clash yet: the battle to claim the entire continent as their own.

In 1753, a young Virginia-born soldier named George Washington was ordered to venture into a French camp to establish whether the French had any intention of leaving Virginia. Promoted for his efforts, Major George Washington returned a year later with 150 troops and built Fort Necessity, from which he took on the French forces. Despite being overwhelmed in 1754, Washington returned to Virginia a hero.

In the war that ensued, the French, though outnumbered, had the advantage of support from the Native Americans, motivated by the chance to rid themselves of the British menace. Fighting was vicious on both sides and, until 1756, went in France's favor. When William Pitt became British prime minister in 1757, the tide turned. The war, known in Europe as the Seven Years' War, became global: Pitt engaged French forces in Europe and in West African and French Indian colonies, gradually wearing down France's imperial ambitions and weakening its international standing.

By the end of the war in 1763, the British controlled North America east of the Mississippi as well as Canada, and gave French Louisiana to Spain in exchange for Florida.

REVOLUTIONARY
AMERICA

KING GEORGE'S PROCLAMATION LINE
1763

Although the French and Indian War ended in victory for the British, it left Britain almost bankrupt and King George III keen not to antagonize the Native Americans into further costly conflicts.

In the latter years of the war, several treaties had been signed between the British and the Native Americans. The 1758 Treaty of Easton, for example, forbade the Native Americans from fighting on the side of the French, and the British from settling on British-controlled Native American land west of the Appalachian Mountains. These treaties were largely ignored, however, and battle-worn settlers continued to head westward to lay claim to the territory they had long fought to control.

But George III was determined to honor the treaties and stabilize relations with the Native Americans. In 1763, a royal proclamation enforced the so-called "Proclamation Line," which ran from Maine to Georgia and outlawed white settlement beyond the crest of the Appalachian Mountains.

There were already many settlements beyond the mountains and it was not long before both frontiersmen and settlers grew impatient and defied the proclamation to cross the mountains. This led to numerous clashes with the Native Americans, but colonial officials refused to help anyone who had violated the Proclamation Line. Eventually, Sir William Johnson, a New Yorker married to an Iroquois woman, began to negotiate for land with the various tribes, and western settlement grew thick and fast. Alienation from Britain increased as bonds between the East Coast and the western settlers grew stronger, and the Proclamation Line eventually sank into obscurity.

THE TYRANNY OF TAXATION
1764–66

The French and Indian War of 1754–63 left Britain with hefty national debts. The British government decided it was only right that the colonies be made to shoulder some of these costs.

Chancellor of the Exchequer George Grenville was instrumental in pushing through the first Act of Parliament specifically designed to raise money from the colonists: the Sugar Act of 1764 imposed taxes on commodities—including sugar and molasses—imported into the colonies. At around the same time, the Currency Act forbade the colonies from issuing their own paper money, thus ensuring that they remained economically dependent upon Britain.

The colonists were furious and, in protest, began to boycott British imports. Their protests were ignored, however, and, in 1765, Parliament wielded its power once more by passing the Quartering Act, which demanded colonists house royal troops in taverns and inns at their own expense. Worse was to follow when, in March 1765, the Stamp Act required that taxes be paid on all paper goods, including legal documents, newspapers and playing cards.

Without any representation within British Parliament, the colonists felt their rights as British subjects were being violated. Protests multiplied, the boycott of British goods continued, and "No taxation without representation" became a common cry. The Stamp Act and the Sugar Act were eventually repealed in 1766, while the Quartering Act was largely defied, but the damage to colonial relations had been done.

THE SONS OF LIBERTY
1765–74

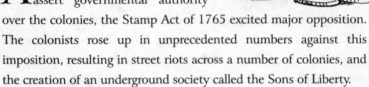

As the first significant attempt to assert governmental authority over the colonies, the Stamp Act of 1765 excited major opposition. The colonists rose up in unprecedented numbers against this imposition, resulting in street riots across a number of colonies, and the creation of an underground society called the Sons of Liberty.

Originating in Boston, the Sons of Liberty boasted members from the upper ranks of colonial society down to humble shopkeepers. Their common aim: to resist British-imposed taxes. Holding large public demonstrations in order to spread their views and expand their membership, the Sons organized the boycotting of British goods and targeted the tax collectors. On one occasion, an effigy of newly appointed stamp commissioner Andrew Oliver was burned and his home in Boston ransacked. He resigned within days.

The repeal of the Stamp Act achieved the Sons' first objective, but with other British taxes to oppose, it was not long before Sons of Liberty sprang up in every colony. In 1767, they coordinated a blockade of British goods in response to the Townshend Acts, which were a collection of new taxes on a number of popular commodities including tea, designed in part to offset the costs of the Seven Years' War. Many members of the society, including Paul Revere, Samuel Adams and John Adams, went on to become leaders of the Revolution.

THE BOSTON MASSACRE
March 5, 1770

With relations between Britain and the colonists having soured following quarrels over taxes and customs regulations, tensions escalated further when the British government sent troops into Boston in 1768. They were charged with keeping the peace, but also with enforcing the unpopular Townshend Acts, and there were frequent angry clashes between troops and colonists.

Anger turned to bloodshed in May of that year, when Private Hugh White, a British sentry stationed outside the Custom House, became involved in a brawl with a barber's apprentice. The ensuing skirmish attracted more citizens to the scene, and the soldier soon found himself surrounded by an agitated mob. A squad of "redcoats"—British soldiers—led by Captain Thomas Preston came to his aid, and, in the commotion, fired a number of shots into the crowd. Three civilians died instantly; two more died as a result of their wounds.

Captain Preston and six of his men were tried for murder. Given the incendiary nature of the incident, noted lawyer and future president John Adams, though a staunch Patriot—a rebel against the British—agreed to Preston's plea to act as defense counsel in order to ensure a fair trial. Preston was acquitted but two of the redcoats were found guilty of manslaughter.

The Boston Massacre, as it became known, fueled anti-British propaganda and brought America one step closer to revolution.

THE BOSTON TEA PARTY
December 16, 1773

By the late eighteenth century, tea was Britain's most valuable export. To capitalize on its popularity in America, British Parliament upheld the tax on imported tea that it had incorporated into the Townshend Acts, long after the other Townshend taxes had been repealed.

With smuggling and the boycotting of British goods rife, Britain's biggest tea producer, the East India Company, fell on hard times. To revive its fortunes, Parliament passed the Tea Act in 1773, authorizing the East India Company to trade directly with the colonies rather than via London. Bypassing the London import tax allowed the company to undercut the prices charged by colonial merchants and smugglers, effectively monopolizing the American market.

The colonists were outraged by this underhand attempt to force them into favoring British produce and decreed a boycott of British tea. When three East India Company ships docked in Boston Harbor in November 1773, angry protestors prevented the tea from being unloaded and demanded the ships return to Britain. The British-appointed governor of Massachusetts ordered a blockade of the harbor until the tea was unloaded and the import tax paid, and a standoff ensued.

On December 16, 1773, members of the Sons of Liberty, disguised as Native Americans, boarded the ships and dumped the contents of 342 tea chests—worth around $1.8 million in today's currency—into Boston Harbor. As news of the protest spread, other seaports staged their own "tea parties," and Parliament reacted with a new series of restrictive legislation.

THE INTOLERABLE ACTS
1774

The Intolerable Acts—or the Coercive Acts, as they were officially termed—were British Parliament's harsh response to the Boston Tea Party debacle. They were designed to break the rebellious tension that had been mounting in Massachusetts for a decade, and to serve as a warning to the colonies against opposing British rule.

Under the terms of four of the five acts, Boston was hit particularly hard: Boston Port was shut down until the cost of the tea destroyed during the Boston Tea Party was recovered, the Massachusetts capital was moved to Salem, and Marblehead became the official port of entry. Within the wider colony, a considerable number of elected officials were replaced by members appointed by the king, town meetings without royal approval were banned, and any legal trials involving British subjects were liable to be moved to another colony, or even to Britain. Royal troops were permitted to requisition houses or empty buildings if barracks were unavailable.

The fifth act, the Quebec Act, expanded that province's borders and granted religious freedom to its Roman Catholics, in the hope of ensuring Quebec's allegiance to Britain at a time of increasing American rebellion.

Parliament had hoped the new laws would quell colonial disobedience and bring the colonies back under its control. It could not have been more wrong. Americans of all political persuasions felt their liberty was under serious threat and united for the first time against Britain.

THE FIRST CONTINENTAL CONGRESS
1774

In September 1774, twelve of the thirteen colonies sent delegates to Carpenter's Hall, Philadelphia, for the First Continental Congress. Peyton Randolph, Speaker of Virginia's House of Burgesses, chaired the meeting; other eminent attendees included George Washington and John Adams. The Congress's main purpose was to discuss the colonies' reactions to the Intolerable Acts, and to settle upon a united response.

Of the fifty-six delegates who attended, opinions were evenly divided between radicals who were prepared to fight for separation from Britain, and loyalist representatives who favored a resolution. But they were all agreed on three main objectives: to produce a declaration of rights and grievances; to identify Parliament's abuse of these rights; and to come up with a plan of action that would persuade Parliament to acknowledge these rights.

A "Plan of Union of Great Britain and the Colonies" proposed by Pennsylvania suggested that an elected Grand Council, acting as an equivalent to British Parliament, would represent colonial interests, along with a Crown-appointed president-general who would represent the king's interests. Congress voted narrowly against this plan, but lauded the more radical "Suffolk Resolves" drawn up by colonists from Massachusetts in response to their particularly harsh penalization under the terms of the Intolerable Acts.

Passed on September 17, 1774, the Resolves decreed a boycott of all British goods until the Intolerable Acts were repealed. They listed a number of terms specific to Massachusetts, but the other colonies imposed nonimportation policies in a show of solidarity. Parliament reacted swiftly and declared the American colonies to be in rebellion.

THE BATTLE OF CONCORD
April 19, 1775

Following resolutions made at the First Continental Congress, colonial Patriots prepared themselves for conflict and formed special units known as Minutemen, made up of younger militiamen trained for swift deployment and high mobility.

Meanwhile, British General Thomas Gage was authorized to use force against the colonists and sent 700 British troops, commanded by Lieutenant-Colonel Francis Smith, to seize and destroy military supplies stored in Concord, Massachusetts. But he hadn't bargained on the intelligence-gathering powers of the Patriots, who had been forewarned and had already moved the supplies.

On April 18, 1775, Paul Revere, a leader of the Sons of Liberty, rode through the night from Charlestown, Massachusetts, to Lexington to warn of the approach of British troops. He carried on toward Concord and was captured by a British patrol, but not before drawing dozens of other riders to his cause and ensuring the warning was passed on. His heroic journey was immortalized in Henry Wadsworth Longfellow's 1863 poem "Paul Revere's Ride."

Following a confrontation at Lexington in which a number of Americans were killed, British soldiers reached Concord on April 19 to find several hundred Minutemen positioned on the far side of the North Bridge. The first shot fired by Patriots was described by Ralph Waldo Emerson in his "Concord Hymn" as the "shot heard 'round the world." The Revolutionary War had begun.

British troops eventually retreated under gunfire to Boston. Years of warfare lay ahead, but the Battle of Concord demonstrated the Americans' determination and skill at arms.

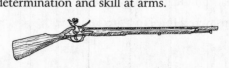

THE BATTLE OF BUNKER HILL
June 17, 1775

After the Battle of Concord, British troops were held under siege in Boston by colonial militia controlling all land access into the city. The waters surrounding Boston, however, were dominated by British warships, enabling besieged troops to be reinforced and resupplied. Thus strengthened, the British offered an amnesty to all colonists except chief agitators Sam Adams and John Hancock, although they were never seized.

In response, the Massachusetts Committee of Safety—which organized the local militia and was led by John Hancock—decided to hasten the progress of the siege by securing a position from which to bombard Boston. Colonial forces, led by newly appointed commander in chief George Washington, were directed to fortify Bunker Hill on Charlestown Heights, overlooking Boston Harbor, an ill-advised move considering their guns were not capable of reaching Boston from that distance. A further misjudgment occurred when a change in tactics led to the fortification of Breed's Hill instead, which, although closer to Boston, was lower and more vulnerable.

After learning of militia activity, 2,500 British troops commanded by General William Howe launched an attack on Breed's Hill. Numbering less than half the British, the colonists nonetheless managed to repel the first two assaults. A third offensive only succeeded after the colonists ran out of ammunition.

Although the colonists were defeated at Bunker Hill—misnamed for the position that *should* have been defended—the British suffered the heaviest losses: a staggering 42 percent of their troops were killed. The battle had proved beyond all doubt that the less experienced colonial troops were a force to be reckoned with.

THE DECLARATION OF INDEPENDENCE
July 4, 1776

By 1776, the American Revolution was well under way, but not all colonists favored independence. The Second Continental Congress had convened in May 1775 and sent an "Olive Branch Petition" to King George III in the hope that he would redress the colonists' grievances and re-establish good relations with Britain. Written by Thomas Jefferson of Virginia and John Dickinson of Pennsylvania, the Petition was duly rejected by the king, who issued a "Proclamation of Rebellion" indicating that he would consider "friendly offers of foreign assistance" in suppressing the American revolt.

In January 1776, Thomas Paine, a radical British intellectual who had emigrated to America, published his pamphlet *Common Sense*, strongly advocating independence. It sold 120,000 copies in three months, public sentiment in favor of independence strengthened, and the thirteen colonies united as never before. In June, the Continental Congress appointed five of its members—among them John Adams, Thomas Jefferson, and Benjamin Franklin—to draft the most important document in American history.

On July 1, this "Declaration of Independence," written by Jefferson in seventeen days, was presented to Congress. It stated "That these united Colonies are, and of Right ought to be Free and Independent States, that they are Absolved from all Allegiance to the British Crown, and that all political connection between them and the State of Great Britain, is and ought to be totally dissolved."

Congress approved the document's wording on July 4, which continues to be celebrated as Independence Day.

EARLY SUCCESSES AND FAILURES
1776

The Declaration of Independence was a vital development in the Revolutionary War, unifying the American colonies under one cause, but Britain was not prepared to concede its colonies so easily, and the fighting continued for another five years. The Declaration did, however, come at the end of a very good year for the American forces. Their capture of Dorchester Heights in March 1776 effectively ended the Siege of Boston, and the British evacuated by sea and established new headquarters in Halifax, Nova Scotia.

In the meantime, British plans to subdue the Southern rebellion in its infancy had been thwarted. In February 1776, Patriot forces defeated Scottish Loyalists in North Carolina; in June, General Sir Henry Clinton's attack on Fort Sullivan in Charleston, South Carolina, was an unmitigated disaster, not least because he had gravely underestimated the Patriots' strength and determination. British activity in the South was more or less halted for the next two years.

It was a different story in the North. America's attempt to enlist the support of the French in recently conquered Quebec failed when Patriot troops were run out of the province. At the same time, General Howe launched a massive attack on New York. George Washington and his Continental Army were defeated in Long Island in August, and again in November in Manhattan. It was no simple victory for the British, however: Washington put up a spirited fight that cost Howe men, money, and time.

TRENTON, SARATOGA, AND PHILADELPHIA
1777

By winter 1776, the British had taken New York and American morale was low. Convinced that the Patriots were all but defeated, General Howe decided to send his army into winter quarters; only a threadbare line of Hessians—German mercenaries—was left to guard the banks of the Delaware. On Christmas Day, Washington made the bold move that was to elevate his reputation: He crossed the Delaware to Trenton, New Jersey, under cover of darkness and defeated the Hessians in a surprise attack. He followed this with another victory at Princeton on January 3, 1777. Both successes boosted American morale and convinced Congress to reject the latest British peace terms, which would have granted the Americans greater autonomy under British rule.

Further Patriot successes followed near Saratoga, New York, when British forces were defeated at the battles of Freeman's Farm and Bemis Heights in September and October 1777. British General John Burgoyne and his entire army of some 6,000 men surrendered to the Patriots on October 17, 1777.

General Howe, in the meantime, advanced toward Pennsylvania determined to take Philadelphia, the home of the Continental Congress. He finally succeeded on September 26, 1777. But victory was hollow, since Congress simply decamped to York, Pennsylvania. Although the Patriots were defeated in an attempt to retake Philadelphia in the Battle of Germantown on October 4, their courage impressed the French to such an extent that a Franco-American alliance was formed on February 6, 1778. France became the first nation to recognize the "United States of America."

THE ARTICLES OF CONFEDERATION
March 1, 1781

The Declaration of Independence was a heartfelt document with truly honorable objectives, but it failed to find a way in which the separate colonies, all acting under their own individual authority, could unite under a single government. In trying to address this flaw the Continental Congress, after much debate, finally drafted the Articles of Confederation, a constitution governing the alliance of thirteen colonies that was now known as the "United States of America."

The colonies were understandably mistrustful of a central government with too much power. The strong British government had, after all, historically ignored their wishes, and it was "taxation without representation" that had led them into the Revolutionary War.

With this in mind, the Articles—effectively agreed upon in November 1777 although not officially ratified until March 1781— established a "firm league of friendship" between the thirteen states and called for a committee made up of delegates from each state. These individuals would constitute a confederation government whose responsibilities would include maintaining an army and navy, making decisions on foreign affairs, and declaring war and peace. The largest share of power, however, was to go to the individual states, each one able to levy its own taxes and retain its own "sovereignty, freedom and independence."

The Articles, though only a temporary solution, were a vital early constitution and held the colonies together for the remainder of the Revolutionary War that was still being fought. They were replaced by the United States Constitution in 1788.

LAST YEARS AND VICTORY AT YORKTOWN
1778–81

A merica's Continental Army survived the terrible winter of 1778, and by spring it had both new recruits and the promise of military assistance from France.

In the wake of the Franco-American alliance, fighting had spread to Britain's colonies in the West Indies. The British also turned their attention back to the South, sweeping down the coast notching up one victory after another, including the capture of Savannah at the Battle of Brewton Hill on December 29, 1778. Fighting continued along the Georgia-South Carolina border throughout 1779, and the Continentals were forced into a humiliating surrender at the Siege of Charleston. In August 1780, General Lord Cornwallis, now in command of British Southern forces, scored a victory at Camden, South Carolina; the coastal South was now in British hands.

While the main battles were being fought, American frontier guerrillas were making their own gains in a series of skillful moves. The Battle of King's Mountain in October 1780 saw 1,000 Loyalist troops crushed; Cornwallis, constantly outmaneuvered by guerrilla tactics, withdrew to the peninsula port of Yorktown, Virginia, in the hope of keeping possession of the South.

General Washington had by this time teamed up with the French army of the Comte de Rochambeau and together, on October 6, 1781, they laid siege to Yorktown. A French fleet prevented the British from escaping by sea, and General Cornwallis surrendered on October 19. America had won the Revolutionary War; the Treaty of Paris, signed in 1783—seven years after the declaration of American independence—marked Britain's official capitulation.

THE BIRTH OF THE UNITED STATES

BETSY ROSS AND THE FIRST STARS AND STRIPES FLAG
1776

Born into a Pennsylvania Quaker family in 1752, Betsy Griscom was the eighth of seventeen children. Upon completing her education at a Quaker public school, Betsy was apprenticed to a local upholsterer, where she soon excelled in all manner of sewing commissions, including flag making. It was here that she met her first husband, John Ross, an Episcopalian. When the couple eloped to New Jersey, Betsy was disowned by her family and "read out" of the Quaker community.

The newlyweds started their own upholstery business and worshipped at the Episcopalian Christ Church in Philadelphia, where Betsy would often sit in a pew adjacent to George Washington, the new commander in chief of the Continental Army.

Both John Ross and Betsy's second husband, Joseph Ashburn, died in the Revolutionary War, but she maintained her respected upholstery business; indeed, according to family lore, Washington was a regular customer. Betsy later recalled a day in May 1776 when Washington, landowner Robert Morris and Colonel George Ross—her first husband's uncle—came to see her. She was shown the rough design of a flag and greatly impressed the men when she demonstrated how she could "cut a five-pointed star in a single snip." Betsy is said to have sewn the very first "stars and stripes" flag: thirteen stripes alternating red and white, representing the thirteen American colonies, and a circle of thirteen stars, white on a blue field, "representing a new constellation."

THE UNITED STATES CONSTITUTION
March 4, 1789

The United States Constitution is the oldest federal constitution in the world. It succeeded the Articles of Confederation as America's governing document, changing the style of government from confederation to federal; that is, from an alliance of self-governing states to a nation unified by its fundamental principles and elected government, under which the states retained certain individual rights.

The inherent weakness of Congress under the Articles of Confederation became abundantly evident in 1786, when Daniel Shays led mobs of beleaguered war veterans and farmers, impoverished by a debt crisis in Massachusetts, in an attack on the state government. "Shays' Rebellion" seriously disrupted local debt-collection hearings, but Congress was powerless to intervene.

In May 1787, fifty-five state representatives gathered in Philadelphia for the Constitutional Convention, and two plans emerged. The Virginia Plan proposed a central federal government with a House and a Senate, an executive chosen by the legislature, and a judiciary. It favored the larger states, with representation proportionate to population. The New Jersey Plan favored keeping most of the Articles of Confederation and allowing all states equal representation. It recommended a Supreme Court and no executive branch.

When debate became heated, the "Great Compromise" was negotiated: The House would represent the people, the Senate would represent the states, and an Electoral College, to which each state contributed a number of "electors" proportionate to its population, would elect a president. The Constitution became law on June 21, 1788, and was officially put into effect on March 4, 1789, with George Washington unanimously elected president.

THE BILL OF RIGHTS
1789

Introduced to the First Congress of the United States in September 1789 and ratified in December 1791, the Bill of Rights addressed public concern about the extent of the federal government's power.

First Amendment: Protects freedom of speech, religion, and the press, and protects "the right of the people peaceably to assemble, and to petition the Government for a redress of grievances."

Second Amendment: Protects "the right of the people to keep and bear Arms."

Third Amendment: Prohibits the quartering of troops in private houses in peacetime "without the consent of the Owner."

Fourth Amendment: Prohibits "unreasonable searches and seizures."

Fifth Amendment: Requires indictment by grand jury for an "infamous crime," protects against double jeopardy and self-incrimination, and prohibits the taking of life, liberty, or property "without due process of law."

Sixth Amendment: Guarantees a defendant "a speedy and public trial, by an impartial jury," full information on "the nature and cause of the accusation," and the right "to be confronted with the witnesses against him, and have the Assistance of Counsel for his defence."

Seventh Amendment: Guarantees "the right of trial by jury."

Eighth Amendment: Prohibits "excessive bail," "excessive fines," and "cruel and unusual punishments."

Ninth Amendment: "The enumeration in the Constitution, of certain rights, shall not be construed to deny or disparage others."

Tenth Amendment: Clarifies that "powers not delegated to the United States by the Constitution, nor prohibited by it to the States" are reserved to the states or the people.

BENJAMIN FRANKLIN AND THE FOUNDING FATHERS
January 17, 1706–April 17, 1790

B enjamin Franklin was born into the family of a Boston candle-
and soap-maker. Despite a brief education, he displayed an early
precociousness, becoming a popular correspondent to his brother's
paper, *The New-England Courant*, at the age of fifteen. Two years later,
he ran away to Philadelphia and established himself as a printer.

In 1729, Franklin became the publisher of the successful
Pennsylvania Gazette, and began his lifetime devotion to "the greater
good." He was instrumental in founding the Library Company
of Philadelphia—a subscription library, public hospitals, fire
departments, and the American Philosophical Society, a discussion
group whose members included George Washington and Thomas
Paine. From 1732 to 1758 Franklin published the annual *Poor
Richard's Almanack*, containing everything from weather forecasts
to new aphorisms (a favorite of Franklin's being "Time is money"),
while his considerable scientific curiosity led him to develop, among
other things, the lightning rod, swim fins, and bifocals.

Franklin had always been interested in politics, and went on to
serve as an ambassador to France. He was a key player in persuading
the French to side with America during the Revolutionary War,
and was a signatory of the Treaty of Paris at the end of it. A skilled
diplomat, Franklin was chosen to represent Philadelphia at the Second
Continental Congress, where, as part of a group of political leaders
known today as the Founding Fathers, he co-drafted and signed the
Declaration of Independence, and later signed the Constitution.

Franklin's *Memoirs* were incomplete when he died in Philadelphia
at age eighty-four, but were subsequently published to great acclaim.

GEORGE WASHINGTON
February 22, 1732–December 14, 1799

George Washington was born in Virginia and brought up on his father's plantation. A surveyor by the time he was sixteen, Washington helped map out Belhaven, Virginia, and inherited part of the family estate at Mount Vernon in 1752.

He served in the early years of the French and Indian War and had been promoted to major by the age of twenty. Resigning from military service in 1758, Washington returned home to manage his estate and to serve in the early Virginian governing body, the Burgesses. The following year, he embarked on a happy and fortuitous marriage to wealthy widow Martha Custis, and became the richest man in Virginia.

Like many of his fellow colonists, Washington felt hampered by Britain's oppressive policies. He was selected to represent Virginia at the Continental Congress, which elected him commander in chief of the Continental Army in May 1775. Washington proved an exceptional leader and strategist throughout six grueling years of war.

Washington played a major role in the lead-up to the Constitutional Convention of 1787; when the Constitution and new federal government were ratified in 1789, the Electoral College unanimously voted him first president of the United States. His greatest achievement was to establish America as a nation in its own right, and the new federal capital founded in 1790 was named after him.

Washington retired to Mount Vernon after two terms (setting an unofficial precedent for length of service) and was bestowed with the title "Father of His Country." He died of a throat infection less than three years later.

JOHN ADAMS
October 30, 1735–July 4, 1826

B orn into a prominent Massachusetts family, John Adams was a gifted scholar. He went to Harvard at sixteen and became a respected lawyer whose rallying response to the Stamp Act of 1765 brought him into the political sphere. Adams was the first advocate of independence at the Second Continental Congress, and established vital diplomatic relations with Europe during the Revolutionary War, setting up the first American embassy abroad, in the Netherlands.

In 1789, Adams was elected first vice president of the United States. He kept up an appearance of support for President Washington's policies, establishing a benchmark for future vice presidents, despite privately condemning the role as "the most insignificant office ever conceived."

Elected president in 1796 upon Washington's resignation, Adams was the first resident of what is now called the White House. Foreign affairs became his immediate priority when France—angered by Washington's refusal to collude in a war against Britain—engaged in attacks on American merchant ships. The failure of diplomatic negotiations led to two years of undeclared naval warfare with France (known as the Quasi-War), and weakened Adams's reputation at home. Fearing revolution, he introduced the Alien and Sedition Acts of 1798, cracking down on both immigration and criticism of the government. His key opponents, including Thomas Jefferson and James Madison, were enraged, and he was ousted from power in the presidential campaign of 1800.

Embittered, Adams retired to Massachusetts, but resumed a friendly correspondence with Jefferson a decade later. He died shortly after his son John Quincy Adams became the nation's sixth president.

FEDERALISTS V. REPUBLICANS: THE PRESIDENTIAL CAMPAIGN OF 1800

By the time George Washington retired in 1796, two camps had emerged from the debate on how the United States should best be governed, although they had not yet formed distinct political parties. On one side were the Federalists, who believed that the country should be steered by a strong central, or federal, government. On the other were the Republicans, who favored a system under which the states would govern themselves.

When John Adams was elected Washington's Federalist successor, he was faced with the crisis of political division within a government that had so recently seemed unified in its vision, not least because his vice president was leading Republican Thomas Jefferson. His Sedition Act effectively violated the First Amendment by outlawing public opposition to the government. The Republican press was naturally hardest hit, prompting Jefferson and James Madison to attack the ban in the Virginia and Kentucky legislatures. They called on the Supreme Court to protect free speech, and on states to invalidate any act of Congress deemed to violate the Constitution.

The presidential election of 1800 was fought in the press, with slander and gutter journalism setting the tone. The Republicans campaigned hard, mobilizing support with pamphlets and mass meetings. The bitter taste of Adams's dubious policies garnered support for the Republicans and, although New England remained predominantly Federalist, Jefferson and the Republicans triumphed.

Adams and the Federalists accepted defeat graciously, and the precedent of a peaceful transition between two presidents—and two political parties—was established.

THOMAS JEFFERSON
April 13, 1743–July 4, 1826

Thomas Jefferson was born in Virginia. He went to school in Williamsburg, later remaining there to study law, and became a lawyer in 1767.

After two years of legal practice, Jefferson realized his passion for politics, and was elected to Virginia's House of Burgesses. He officially abandoned law in 1774, and, alongside George Washington, was a Virginian delegate to the Continental Congress. Respected as a political writer, he was called upon to draft the Declaration of Independence in 1776.

Jefferson spent much of the 1780s as an American envoy in pre-Revolutionary Paris, and became Washington's secretary of state upon his return. It was during Jefferson's tenure that the United States made its first move toward neutral foreign policy. As Jefferson declared after winning the presidency in 1800, "Peace, commerce, and friendship with all nations, entangling alliances with none."

The first Republican Party was a legacy of Jefferson's opposition to his Federalist predecessor, John Adams. In 1798, while serving as Adams's vice president, Jefferson drafted the Kentucky Resolutions, promoting states' rights and the disempowerment of central federal government. As president, he restricted federal economic control, cut government jobs, and slashed the size of the standing army and navy. In terms of religious freedom, Jefferson was the most radical of all the Founding Fathers, famously saying that another man's religious conviction "neither picks my pocket nor breaks my leg."

Jefferson retired in 1808 and worked toward the founding of the University of Virginia. He lived to see its inauguration in 1825 and died the following year, on Independence Day.

MARBURY V. MADISON AND THE POWER OF THE SUPREME COURT
1803

In the final days of his presidency, Federalist John Adams sought to undermine the imminent "revolution" heralded by Republican Thomas Jefferson's election. He packed the Supreme Court with "Midnight Judges," who tirelessly swore in dozens of new judges, all nominated by Adams and hurriedly confirmed by the Senate, and all of fervent Federalist inclination. Adams appointed his outgoing secretary of state, John Marshall, Chief Justice of the Supreme Court.

In 1803, Marshall faced the most important case of his thirty-four-year tenure. President Jefferson's secretary of state, James Madison, had refused to recognize the appointments of some of the Midnight Judges. Four of them promptly sued, including William Marbury, whose case went all the way to the Supreme Court.

Marshall's ruling in the case of *Marbury v. Madison* struck at the heart of the American judiciary. He declared that Secretary of State Madison was violating Marbury's "vested legal right" to his Senate-approved appointment. However, the 1789 Judiciary Act, under which the Supreme Court could have forced Madison to confirm Marbury's appointment, was found to contravene the United States Constitution, under which the Supreme Court had no such power.

Marshall's landmark ruling—that an act of Congress could be invalidated if it was "unconstitutional"—upheld the principle that "a law repugnant to the Constitution is void." He asserted the supremacy of the Constitution over any subsequent law, as well as the Supreme Court's power of judicial review over any act of Congress or state law. "It is, emphatically," he declared, "the province and duty of the judicial department, to say what the law is."

AMERICAN
EXPANSION
AND REFORM

THE LOUISIANA PURCHASE AND THE LEWIS AND CLARK EXPEDITION
1803–06

In 1800, less than forty years after taking control of Louisiana, a weakened Spain was forced by Napoleon to hand the territory back to France. When Jefferson learned of this secret reacquisition, he recognized the threat of a French presence in the Western territories and offered to buy Louisiana. Napoleon acquiesced in May 1803 and sold the territory for $15 million, money he badly needed to fund ongoing conflicts in Europe. The Louisiana Purchase doubled the size of the United States, whose Western border now stretched from New Orleans to the top of modern-day Montana.

The exact size of Louisiana was unclear to both the French and the Americans at the time of the Purchase, so Jefferson persuaded Congress to fund a scientific and commercial expedition into the West to discover and chart what exactly America now owned.

In the winter of 1803, Captain Meriwether Lewis and Second Lieutenant William Clark of the US Army were dispatched at the head of an arduous expedition to the Western border, and to see what lay beyond it. They were charged with examining wildlife and terrain, assessing the dispositions of Native Americans living beyond Louisiana, and mapping unknown territories. At the end of 1805, the team finally reached the Pacific Coast, whereupon they divided into two groups and charted different routes back. This expedition fed curiosity about the American West, and fueled a growing desire for the United States to stretch to the Pacific.

THE "WAR OF 1812"
1812–15

President Jefferson retained the neutral foreign policy he had championed as Washington's secretary of state, but it was severely tested by British involvement in Napoleon's European wars. Not only did Britain try to prevent free American trade with France, but it also engaged in "impressment," the forceful removal of "British subjects"—British-American immigrants—from mid-Atlantic merchant ships, for immediate enlistment into the British navy. Thousands of American citizens were seized in this way.

After James Madison became president in 1808, strained American-British relations deteriorated further still, and in 1811, the British, who still controlled Canada, supported Native American forces in an attack on America's expanding Northwest frontier (now Ohio, Indiana, Michigan, Illinois and Wisconsin).

America and Britain went to war in June 1812, and fought a series of largely inconclusive battles across America for two and a half years. The end of the Napoleonic Wars in 1814 released 14,000 British troops, who were all swiftly redeployed to the United States. Thus bolstered, British forces marched on Washington, D.C., in the summer of 1814, and set fire to the Executive Mansion.

On Christmas Eve 1814, the two sides signed the Treaty of Ghent, in Belgium. But news of the peace didn't reach America until February 1815, by which time the British had attacked New Orleans. Ironically, this was the only definitive American success of the war, with over 20,000 British casualties. The Treaty restored peace but resolved very little. As the dust settled, the scorched Executive Mansion was painted white, although it was not officially known as the "White House" until 1901.

THE NATIONAL ANTHEM
1814

In September 1814, during the so-
called "War of 1812," Georgetown
lawyer and US Army officer Francis Scott Key
was invited by three notable British officers to dine aboard their
vessel HMS *Tonnant*, anchored in Chesapeake Bay. Key was trying to
secure the release of his friend and colleague Dr. William Beanes, a
prisoner of the British. Preoccupied with the imminent bombardment
of Baltimore and Fort William, the British officers eventually agreed
to let Dr. Beanes go, and returned the Americans to their sailboat.
They were kept under guard in the harbor, however, to prevent any
information about British military strategy from becoming public.

When the Battle of Baltimore began, Key had no choice but to
observe the bombardment from his vantage point in the harbor. He
watched with pride as American forces successfully defended Fort
McHenry, and was moved to see the Stars and Stripes flag flying
through the rain and smoke. Inspired by American victory in the
face of the mighty British navy, Key composed a poem honoring "the
land of the free and the home of the brave," which he scrawled onto
the back of a letter.

Within a week, "The Defence of Fort McHenry" had been set
to the tune of an old British drinking song and printed in national
newspapers. It was adopted by President Hoover as the National
Anthem in 1931, and is now popularly known as "The Star-Spangled
Banner."

THE MOUNTAIN MEN
1810–40

The legendary frontiersmen, or "mountain men," were hardy, courageous, and adept at surviving in the wilderness. They roamed the Great Plains and North American Rocky Mountains between around 1810 and 1840, charting previously unknown territory, hunting, trapping, and trading in fur.

There were two regions of trade: the Upper Missouri, where Native American tribes brought buffalo skins to trading posts, and the Rocky Mountains, where mountain men, employed by companies such as the Rocky Mountain Fur Company, trapped beaver and sold the pelts at a yearly rendezvous. This arrangement meant that the hunters lived in the wilderness year-round, facing the constant perils of starvation, cold, wild animals, and hostile Native Americans.

The fur trade fell into decline when the fashion for beaver hats died out, and a number of frontiersmen used their knowledge and experience to become guides, explorers, and Native American agents (middlemen between the Native Americans and the government).

Many mountain men emerged as notable historical figures. Daniel Boone was one of the early frontiersmen; his adventures pioneering the exploration of Kentucky turned him into the archetypal Western hero of American folklore. Davy Crockett, "King of the Wild Frontier," was also a Native American fighter and politician. He represented Tennessee in the House of Representatives and died at the Battle of the Alamo. Jim Bridger gained renown for "discovering" the Great Salt Lake in 1824 and later finding what became known as Bridger's Pass, a considerable shortcut on the Oregon Trail.

THE MISSOURI COMPROMISE
1820

By 1818, when Missouri petitioned Congress for admission to the Union, the issue of slavery had become highly contentious. For decades, the balance between Northern free states and Southern slave states had been precariously maintained, with twenty-two free-state senators and twenty-two slave-state senators sitting in Congress at the time of the petition. Missouri, however, was a slave state; by admitting it to the Union, the balance of power would be upset.

James Tallmadge, Jr., a representative of New York, proposed an amendment to the statehood bill: The 2,000 slaves already in Missouri would remain slaves; any further slavery would be banned; and any children born slaves would be freed at the age of twenty-five. In this way, slavery would gradually be eradicated from Missouri. A complicated and drawn-out debate ensued, in which Northern senators asserted that Congress would be acting within its rights to ban slavery in any new state, while Southern senators maintained that they had the same right as the original thirteen states to make their own decisions regarding slavery.

In March 1820, following a petition from Maine for admission to the Union, a compromise was finally reached. Maine was admitted as a free state while Missouri was admitted as a slave state, and so the balance was maintained. In a bid to address the future spread of slavery, a line—the Missouri Compromise Line—was drawn across the Louisiana territory; all states north of the line, except for Missouri, would forever remain slave-free.

THE MONROE DOCTRINE
1823

On December 2, 1823, President James Monroe set out America's diplomatic ideals and foreign policy in an address to Congress that became known as the Monroe Doctrine.

The Napoleonic Wars of 1803–15 had encroached upon South America, and the resulting turmoil had provided the opportunity for nationalistic revolutions in Latin America. But when the wars ended, both the United States and the United Kingdom feared that Spain would try to reclaim its empire. South America, newly opened to trade, had proven a prosperous market for British goods; if Spain reclaimed its colonies, that market would be closed off.

British Foreign Minister George Canning suggested that the United States and the United Kingdom join forces to repel any possible interference in South America. Monroe rejected the proposal, and, in a bold and strategic stance against further military intervention, responded with the following doctrine:

The American continents (North and South) were no longer to be considered subjects for future colonization by any European powers.

The political system of the United States was to be recognized as completely different from those of European powers.

The United States would regard any interference by a European power in the affairs of the American continents as an act of aggression and a threat to security.

The United States would no longer participate in European wars or interfere with existing colonies or their dependencies.

The Monroe Doctrine became one of the longest-standing principles of American foreign policy, and was still a subject of great debate during the Cuban Communist Revolution of the late 1950s.

ANDREW JACKSON
March 15, 1767–June 8, 1845

Andrew Jackson was born in South Carolina to Irish immigrants. His education and childhood were brief: By the age of fourteen, he was both an orphan and a veteran of the Revolutionary War. After studying law, he worked as a public prosecutor in an area of North Carolina that later joined Tennessee, and when Tennessee was admitted to the Union in 1796, became its first representative. He distinguished himself in both politics and warfare, serving as major-general in the War of 1812, and was elected to the Senate in 1823.

Jackson's illustrious life was not without controversy: His wife Rachel was not divorced at the time of their marriage, and he fought numerous duels in defense of her honor, once killing his opponent, skilled duelist Charles Dickinson.

Branded a populist "jackass" by opponents, Jackson was elected America's seventh president in 1828, campaigning under the emblem of a stubborn donkey—later the Democratic Party's unofficial symbol—and the slogan "Let the people rule." He embraced greater democracy but was inconsistent, empowering federal government despite believing in individual rights, and attacking his fellow Southern slave owners when his authority was threatened. His well-meaning Indian Removal Act, which encouraged (and in some instances compelled) Native Americans to vacate Southern states in return for specially designated land in the West, resulted in the Trail of Tears tragedy in which thousands died from disease and starvation.

But Jackson's take on the presidential role—from vetoing laws he considered harmful, to asserting himself as the representative of every American—did much to shape the modern presidency. Jackson retired to Tennessee in 1837, and died there eight years later.

THE NULLIFICATION CRISIS
1828–33

In the early years of the nineteenth century, the cotton trade in the Southern states was booming. The United Kingdom in particular was buying huge quantities of raw cotton, turning it into high-quality cloth, and exporting it back to America. With no import duties or tariffs, American customers could easily afford the British cloth, and the profitable business cycle continued. The textile industries of the Northern states, however, found they could not compete.

In 1828, in a bid to persuade American customers to buy domestic products and thereby boost Northern industry, Congress levied a duty on manufactured imports. The Northern states welcomed the move, but this "Tariff of Abominations" was condemned in the South. Vice President John C. Calhoun of South Carolina led the dissent with his essay "South Carolina Exposition and Protest," which demanded the federal tariff be declared "null and void" by any state that deemed it unconstitutional.

President Jackson had promised tariff reforms in his election campaign, but his revised tariff of 1832 still penalized Southern agriculturalists. An incensed Calhoun—who had by now resigned over the issue—called a convention in South Carolina and announced an Ordinance of Nullification, effectively forbidding the collection of duties within that state. Jackson responded by denying any state the right to resist a federal law, and threatened military intervention through the Force Bill of 1833—which South Carolina promptly nullified. The Compromise Tariff, brought in at the same time, eventually pacified the South and, for the time being at least, forestalled a potential civil war.

THE WHIGS
1833–56

By the late 1820s, changes to the voting system had transformed the nature of politics. The vote was no longer dependent on property ownership: Now most states gave every white man a vote. Organized party politics came into play for the first time during Andrew Jackson's presidency, spurred on by national newspapers declaring their political allegiances and publicizing policies on key issues of the day.

The early 1830s saw a growing debate about the appropriate balance of power between local and national government. Under Jackson, the Democratic Party pushed for more power to lie with the executive than with Congress. His opponents decried what they saw as an arrogant assumption of supremacy over Congress—the representatives of the people, after all—and urged Jackson to support a program of national modernization. A national bank and improved interstate roads, railroads, and canals were chief among their demands. This opposition to the high-handed policies of "King Andrew" Jackson solidified in 1833 into the Whig Party, so named because Whigs had traditionally opposed autocratic monarchies in Europe.

The Whigs ran as the nation's second party for just over two decades, with Abraham Lincoln becoming one of their most prominent leaders. The party enjoyed support among wealthy merchants and industrialists in the North, and was irrevocably divided by the slavery question in the mid-1850s, losing its core supporters to the newly formed Republican Party, which argued strongly against the expansion of slavery.

REMEMBER THE ALAMO!
March 6, 1836

In the early 1820s, Stephen F. Austin, the son of an American entrepreneur, led 300 American families to settle in Tejas (Texas) in the Mexican state of Coahuila y Tejas. By 1836, the number of settlers had swelled to over 50,000.

Mexico—which at the time encompassed modern-day Texas and California—had recently won independence from Spain, and was wary of giving the settlers too much autonomy. The colonists soon became frustrated, and dispatched Austin to Mexico City in 1833 to petition President Antonio López de Santa Anna for Texas's right to separate statehood. The plan was rejected, and Austin was arrested and imprisoned. He was released in 1835, disillusioned enough to join the increasingly violent revolt against Santa Anna; the Texas Revolution had begun.

By February 1836, Texan troops had largely expelled the Mexican Army from Texas. Colonel William Travis and a small band of soldiers took a defensive stand at the former Spanish mission San Antonio de Valero, popularly called "Alamo" after the Spanish word for cottonwood, which grew nearby. On March 6, 1836, Santa Anna and his men stormed the Alamo and executed its defenders, including Davy Crockett. Santa Anna hoped his victory would discourage any future acts of rebellion, but 800 Texans overwhelmed 1,250 Mexican troops one month later, spurred on by Major General Sam Houston's battle cry, "Remember the Alamo!"

The Mexicans were eventually defeated at the Battle of San Jacinto. On May 14, Santa Anna signed the Treaty of Velasco, granting the newly named Republic of Texas independence from Mexico.

AT WAR WITH MEXICO
1846–48

When Texas won independence from Mexico in 1836, American expansionists—including President James K. Polk—were eager to admit it to the Union, at the risk of war with Mexico. Others argued against war, and against adding another slave state to the Union. But when it became clear that both the United Kingdom and France were seeking alliance with Texas, the arguing ceased; Texas became an American state on December 29, 1845.

Mexico reacted as predicted: On May 1, 1846, Mexican troops laid siege to Fort Texas on the northern banks of the Rio Grande. American troops marched to the rescue and were victorious at the nearby Battle of Palo Alto one week later. The United States officially declared war on May 13, 1846, and General Stephen Kearny led his "Army of the West" to the Mexican territory of Alta California via Nuevo México. At Apache Canyon, near Santa Fe, a Mexican ambush led by Governor Manuel Armijo failed when his troops, although outnumbering American forces, panicked and dispersed. Kearny passed through the canyon unchallenged, and Nuevo México was occupied without a shot being fired.

With both the United Kingdom and France eyeing up Alta California—which was still held, precariously, by Mexico—Polk offered Mexican President Santa Anna $40 million for the territory. The offer was rudely rebuffed, prompting Polk to stir up rebellious feelings among the territory's American settlers. When US Army Major John C. Frémont led the 1846 Bear Flag Rebellion (so named because the rebels' flag featured a grizzly bear), wresting Alta California from Mexico and creating the short-lived California Republic, Mexico's humiliation was complete.

THE BATTLES OF MONTERREY AND VERACRUZ
September 1846 and March 1847

By September 1846, the Mexican-American War had seen Mexico suffer a number of crushing defeats. General Pedro de Ampudia and his army, stationed outside the fortress town of Monterrey, were ordered to retreat southward to refit before their next engagement with American troops. But Ampudia, knowing his men were restless and hungry for action, stayed put to fight the approaching American forces led by General Zachary Taylor.

The Mexicans held out for three days and brought the American troops to a standstill, but in a final push, General Taylor began a mass shelling of the walls of the city, eventually breaking through the Mexican defenses and winning a surrender on September 24. Taylor did not capitalize on his victory, however, and agreed to an armistice that allowed the Mexicans to evacuate the city. An incensed President Polk asserted that Taylor had no right to negotiate truces, only to "kill the enemy," and General Winfield Scott was brought in as a replacement.

On March 9, 1847, Scott launched an amphibious attack on the fortified city of Veracruz, and laid siege to it for eighteen days. Mexican troops withdrew to the Cerro Gordo canyon with Scott following close on their heels. In a series of bold offensives, the American forces took the cities of Cerro Gordo, Pueblo, and finally the apparently invincible fortress of Chapultepec, overlooking Mexico City. The Treaty of Guadalupe Hidalgo, ratified on March 10, 1848, finally ended the war with Mexico; in 1850, Alta California became the American state of California and Nuevo México the territory of New Mexico.

"MANIFEST DESTINY"
1812–60

By the 1840s, the expansion of the United States was well under way, with the desire to "overspread the continent" evident in the number of settlers blazing a trail westward. This urge to extend boundaries had been formally articulated in an essay written by journalist John O'Sullivan for the *United States Magazine and Democratic Review* in 1845. Advocating the annexation of Texas, he spoke of "the fulfilment of our manifest destiny to overspread the continent allotted by Providence for the free development of our yearly multiplying numbers."

The presidential campaign of 1844 focused on expansion, with the annexations of Texas and of Oregon Country—northwestern territory held jointly by the United States and the United Kingdom—of particular interest. The Democrat James K. Polk campaigned under the slogan "Fifty-four forty or fight," a reference to the line of latitude at Oregon's northern boundary, and was elected over Whig Henry Clay, whose policy on expansion was less clear-cut.

"Manifest Destiny" became a belief and a moral ideal. It held that the divine mission of the United States was to spread freedom, democracy, and political power from one coast to the other. The phrase was used to promote the vision of expansion, its ideology shaped government policy, and the era between 1812 and 1860—when both Texas and Oregon were indeed annexed—became known as "The Age of Manifest Destiny." But as territorial expansion gradually ceased to be America's focus, the phrase came to embody the country's vision of itself as a leader of the free world.

WESTWARD HO!
1846

In the 1840s, large parties of land seekers joined wagon trains westward in order to establish permanent settlements. Two of the most famous of all westward movements were undertaken by the Donner Party and the Mormons.

In 1846, George Donner of Illinois led his family and two others on a wagon train along the well-established California Trail. Taking a risk on an apparent shortcut through what is now Utah, the Donner Party—now numbering almost ninety people—followed a doomed diversion into the difficult terrain of the Sierra Nevada, just as winter set in. They set up camp, but worsening conditions and diminishing supplies prompted fourteen men and women to push on to California to seek help. Seven of the party perished, famously leaving the seven survivors with little choice but to resort to cannibalism.

The following year, around 150 Mormons—members of the Church of Jesus Christ of Latter-day Saints, founded by Joseph Smith in 1830—adopted what became known as the Mormon Trail. In a bid to escape religious persecution in the East, the Mormons headed for the isolated Great Salt Lake Valley, ultimately following the trail first blazed by the Donner Party. Once a new settlement had been established, successive waves of Mormons arrived in the newfound haven, which prospered when gold hunters began following the Mormon Trail toward the West. Salt Lake City, Utah, is still a Mormon stronghold to this day.

STRIKE IT LUCKY: THE GOLD RUSH OF '49
1849

In January 1848, Californian ranch laborer James Marshall discovered what looked like gold lying at the bottom of a millrun. The owner of the ranch, John Sutter, confirmed his suspicions. Within weeks, Sutter's ranch was deserted, his workers lured away by the promise of gold.

As the news spread, an enterprising Mormon, Sam Brannon, came up with a resourceful way of striking it rich. He publicized the discovery of gold in the newspaper he owned, and then walked the streets of San Francisco, yelling, "Gold! Gold from the America River!" The Gold Rush was officially on, and as would-be prospectors left town, Brannon sold them all the gold-digging equipment they could possibly need. Before long, he had made his first million.

By 1849, hundreds of thousands of gold seekers were flooding into California. They walked the California Trail, sailed around Cape Horn, or trekked through the Panama shortcut. Many "49ers" were rewarded when they struck gold—billions of dollars' worth in today's currency—while other, less fortunate prospectors found only hard times, financial ruin, and even death. Tens of thousands of Native Americans also perished during this period, their traditional society and environment destroyed as fortune seekers ravaged the land.

The Gold Rush changed the Californian landscape significantly: New towns and roads were built, new methods of transportation introduced, and a new agricultural wealth developed as prospectors stayed to farm the land.

THE COTTON GIN AND *UNCLE TOM'S CABIN*
1793–1852

By the late 1700s, slavery in the cotton-growing plantations of the South was booming. Although there was growing opposition to the "peculiar institution" of slavery—with countries the world over outlawing the practice—it continued to play a vital role in the South's economy. The North, by contrast, was becoming increasingly intolerant of slavery; colony after colony declared itself slave-free and, in 1787, the Northwest Ordinance banished slavery from the entire Northwest Territory.

In 1793, New Englander Eli Whitney unwittingly ensured the continuance of the Southern slave trade with his invention of the cotton gin. Designed to separate cottonseed from the cotton fiber, it instantly increased production and profit, and in turn led to a greater demand for land on which to grow cotton—and for slaves to grow and pick the crops. Cotton plantations consequently grew ever busier, and the work of the slaves became ever more soul destroying and relentless. By 1860, one in three inhabitants of the fifteen slave states was a slave.

In the meantime, the anti-slavery movement was gaining momentum. In 1852, *Uncle Tom's Cabin*, a novel by a pro-abolition journalist and teacher named Harriet Beecher Stowe, reached deep into the heart of the abolitionist cause. It portrayed the cruel reality of slavery through the character of an African slave, and became the second-best-selling book of the nineteenth century, beaten only by the Bible. It is credited with intensifying the already heated debate about slavery, which ultimately led to the Civil War.

ABRAHAM LINCOLN
February 12, 1809–April 15, 1865

B orn to farming parents in Kentucky, Abraham Lincoln received little in the way of formal education. He later explained, "When I came of age I did not know much. Still somehow, I could read, write, and cipher." The family relocated first to Indiana—partly on account of it being anti-slavery—and later to Illinois.

Lincoln left home in 1831 and canoed to New Salem, Illinois, where he worked as a storekeeper, surveyor, and postmaster, before serving as a captain in the Black Hawk War, a conflict with Native Americans over disputed Midwestern land. He was elected to the state legislature in 1834, and, after teaching himself law, became a respected attorney in Springfield, Illinois.

Following an ill-fated term in the House of Representatives in 1846, Lincoln returned to politics in indignation at the 1854 Kansas-Nebraska Act, which repealed the Missouri Compromise and sanctioned what he called "the monstrous injustice of slavery." He joined the new Republican Party formed by the act's opponents, and demonstrated both his opposition to slavery and his rhetorical flair in his "Lost Speech" and "House Divided Speech," among others, earning him national recognition.

Lincoln was elected America's sixteenth president in 1860. A deeply principled man, he led his country steadfastly through the devastation of the Civil War. He supported the Homestead Act, signed the Emancipation Proclamation, and espoused equality and freedom in his famous Gettysburg Address. When Confederate sympathizer John Wilkes Booth assassinated him at Ford's Theatre in Washington, D.C., in 1865, the nation mourned a man still regarded today as one of the greatest presidents of all time.

THE KANSAS-NEBRASKA ACT
1854

In 1853, following a decade of debate and disagreement regarding the route for a proposed transcontinental railroad, Senator Stephen A. Douglas struck on an idea to guarantee an outcome favorable to his state, Illinois. Douglas had been campaigning for a northern route that used Chicago as a terminus, but needed the support of the Southern states. Hoping to garner Southern popularity, he introduced a bill that ultimately became the Kansas-Nebraska Act, organizing those two territories and assuring their settlers the right to decide by "popular sovereignty" whether or not to allow slavery.

Douglas's bill was bitterly opposed in the North and strongly embraced in the South. It was fiercely debated in Congress—not least because it effectively repealed the Missouri Compromise as well as the Compromise of 1850, which had decreed the slavery status of new land acquired after the Mexican-American War—but was ultimately passed on May 30, 1854.

While Nebraska was expected to vote itself a free state, Kansas was less polarized. Pro-slavery settlers from Missouri flooded into Kansas in order to vote. They won the election but were charged with fraud by anti-slavery settlers; when the latter held a second election, pro-slavery settlers refused to vote. Two opposing legislatures were created, violence and deaths ensued, and the territory soon became known as "Bleeding Kansas."

The issue of slavery had become the focus of political debate and public aggression. The divide in Congress brought the Whig Party to its knees and gave rise to the new Republican Party, while festering North-South hostility paved the way for civil war.

THE ABOLITIONIST MOVEMENT
1750–1865

Widespread objections to slavery had been voiced as early as the 1750s. In 1774, Rhode Island abolished its slave trade, while the Massachusetts Constitution of 1780 proclaimed "All men are born free and equal." Quock Walker, a Massachusetts slave, used this statement to sue for his freedom, and his success led to the abolition of slavery in that state.

The crusade to eradicate slavery across the nation grew, supported by preachers such as Nathaniel Taylor and Lyman Beecher. The resulting wave of religious revivals added momentum to the abolitionist movement. In 1831, radical abolitionist William Lloyd Garrison established his anti-slavery newspaper, *The Liberator*; he co-founded the American Anti-Slavery Society two years later. *The Liberator* demanded the immediate emancipation of all slaves and a change in America's spiritual values.

In 1856, fervent abolitionist John Brown led the Kansas Free Soil Militia into "Bleeding Kansas" to exact revenge on pro-slavery forces—"border ruffians"—who were running riot in the wake of the Kansas-Nebraska Act. During their attack, five unarmed anti-abolitionists were hacked to death with swords in what became known as the Pottawatomie Massacre.

In 1859, Brown led a raid on the federal arms depot at Harpers Ferry, Virginia, hoping to arm slaves and initiate a rebellion. The plan backfired and several people, including a free slave, were killed by Brown's men. The rebels were eventually cornered and captured by federal troops under Colonel Robert E. Lee, and Brown was executed. His pro-abolitionist actions have since been credited with bringing the United States closer to civil war.

FREDERICK DOUGLASS
February 14, 1818–February 20, 1895

B orn a slave in Maryland, Frederick Douglass was initially raised by his grandmother. He worked on a local plantation from the age of six or seven, and was later sent to Baltimore as a servant. It was here, when Douglass was twelve, that his master's wife began secretly teaching him to read, which was strictly forbidden by law, and by her husband when he found out. Undeterred, and impassioned by the power of the written word, Douglass continued to teach himself, helped by local white children. He bought newspapers and books when he could afford them, and was thus exposed to the political and philosophical debates of the period.

Sent back to the plantation at the age of fifteen, Douglass was appalled by the terrible conditions in which slaves lived and worked, and his insubordination sent him to notorious "slave-breaker" Edward Covey, whom Douglass attacked after a series of whippings. In 1838, Douglass escaped to Massachusetts by impersonating a sailor, taking his future wife Anna, a "free black," with him.

In 1845, after becoming involved in abolitionist meetings and in William Lloyd Garrison's Anti-Slavery Society, Douglass published his eloquent and influential anti-slavery exposé, *Narrative of the Life of Frederick Douglass*. The book became a bestseller and gave him the impetus to establish a number of abolitionist newspapers, notably *The North Star*. He was a leading voice in the African American fight for freedom during the Civil War, and later became a passionate champion of women's rights.

Frederick Douglass died a national hero in 1895, and is buried in Rochester, New York.

THE UNDERGROUND RAILROAD
1810–50

The Underground Railroad was a secret network of routes into the Northern states and Canada that was used by Southern slaves escaping to freedom, and was at its busiest in the first half of the nineteenth century. Organized by dedicated abolitionists, the Railroad—"underground" in the sense of covert—was made up of "conductors," who acted as guides for the fugitives, safe houses or "stations" where they could hide, and the slaves, or "passengers," themselves. Traveling by night on foot, in covered wagons, or hidden inside specially constructed wagons, they stopped at safe houses and were provided with food, money, and a place to rest.

By 1850, at least 8,000 people were working on the Railroad, and Harriet Tubman was one of the most courageous of all. Having escaped to freedom herself in 1849 using the North Star as a guide, she risked recapture and her life by repeatedly venturing back into Maryland to lead hundreds of captives to freedom in Pennsylvania.

Southern slave owners did not take kindly to the Underground Railroad and became troubled and incensed by the numbers of escapees; many conductors whose identities became known were subjected to violence and intimidation. In 1850, Congress was persuaded to pass the Fugitive Slave Act, making it a federal crime to assist any escaping slave and spawning a whole new industry of slave catching. The act failed to shut down the Railroad, however, and the network is estimated to have helped 50,000 to 100,000 slaves attain their liberty in the years leading up to the Civil War.

THE DRED SCOTT DECISION
1857

D red Scott was a slave who belonged to US Army surgeon John Emerson of Missouri. When Emerson was posted to slave-free Illinois and Wisconsin, Scott went with him and lived as a slave on "free soil" for many years.

Shortly after returning to Missouri in 1842, Emerson died. Although Scott had never attempted to end his servitude before, he was encouraged by abolitionist friends to file a suit against Emerson's widow for his freedom, claiming that he should be considered a free citizen, having lived for so long in states in which slavery was illegal.

One Missouri jury ruled against Scott, a second ruled in his favor, and the Missouri Supreme Court upheld Mrs. Emerson's appeal. After ten years, the case eventually made its way to the Supreme Court, where, in March 1857, Chief Justice and former slave owner Roger B. Taney upheld the majority decision, ruling that the descendants of Africans—free or enslaved—were not American citizens, and had no right to sue in a federal court. He declared the 1820 Missouri Compromise to be unconstitutional because it violated the Fifth Amendment, which prohibited the government from depriving an individual of his property—including slaves—without due process of law.

The implications and complications of the Dred Scott Decision were far-reaching: If citizens' constitutional right to human "property" was upheld, the government was obliged to protect slavery in every single state. The ruling was at this point met with abhorrence by all opponents of slavery, and civil war became inevitable.

THE LINCOLN-DOUGLAS DEBATES
1858

The Lincoln-Douglas Debates took place during the 1858 campaign for control of the Illinois legislature. Seven debates were held between Democratic incumbent Stephen A. Douglas and Abraham Lincoln for the newly formed Republican Party. They traveled thousands of miles across Illinois, debating in Ottawa, Freeport, Jonesboro, Charleston, Galesburg, Quincy, and Alton. The debates centered on the contentious issue of slavery—attracting huge crowds and reporters from the national newspapers, which printed the debates verbatim—and are remembered as much for their format and eloquence as for the content of the speeches.

The two candidates held widely opposing views on slavery. Douglas was a supporter of states' individual rights, whereas Lincoln believed that allowing each territory to dictate its own policy served only to endorse and perpetuate slavery as an acceptable practice. Douglas attempted to paint Lincoln as a radical "Black Republican" intent on freeing all slaves, raising their status to equality with whites, and inciting civil war. Lincoln denied being a radical, insisting that he did not wish to bring about the political and social equality of the races, but believed nonetheless that every living man had a right to life, liberty, and the fruits of his own labor.

At Freeport, Douglas was cornered into alienating free-soil Northerners as well as pro-slave Southerners with his vague compromise, the Freeport Doctrine, which supported the Dred Scott Decision in theory but popular sovereignty in practice. He was reelected to the Senate, but had ruined his presidential chances. Lincoln, however, emerged from the debates as a serious presidential candidate.

THE PRESIDENTIAL ELECTION OF 1860

With the slavery debate polarizing Americans as never before, the presidential election of 1860 promised to be a fierce battle. The Democrats nominated their forthright pro-slavery spokesman Stephen A. Douglas, while the Republicans, whose policy was a ban on the further spread of slavery, nominated Abraham Lincoln. Having become increasingly visible—and vocal—in the latter 1850s, dedicating much of his political energy to the condemnation of slavery, Lincoln had swiftly been propelled to the forefront of the Republican Party, and was a natural choice of candidate in an election that would focus almost solely on that issue.

Unlike his opponents, Lincoln declined to hold rallies or to give speeches, and his name did not even appear on a number of Southern ballot slips, yet he defeated his rivals—who also included Vice President John C. Breckinridge for the breakaway Southern Democratic Party, and Tom Bell for the Constitutional Party— with 180 electoral votes, at a time when 152 were needed to win. Breckinridge, his nearest rival, received only 72.

Lincoln's immense popularity in the North carried him to power, but his opponents in the Southern states—not a single one of which he had won—were incensed. Threats of secession had preceded the election, but Lincoln's move to the White House finally pushed the most radical Southern states to make an official attempt at splitting from the Union.

THE CIVIL WAR

CONFEDERATE STATES AND SOUTHERN SECESSION
1861

In the months after Lincoln's election, seven Southern slave states fulfilled their preelection threat and broke away from the Union. South Carolina was the first to secede, soon followed by Alabama, Florida, Georgia, Louisiana, Mississippi, and Texas.

In the "lame duck" months before Lincoln's inauguration, President James Buchanan struggled for a compromise to avert crisis, but took no decisive action. By the time of the inauguration, the seven seceding states had formed the Confederate States of America, and elected Jefferson Davis as their president. Davis rejected a Washington-led compromise, regarding any submission as a risk to Southern liberty. The Confederacy adopted a new constitution that defended the right to slave ownership, declaring "the great truth that the Negro is not equal to the white man."

Eight Southern states remained in the Union, and Lincoln cautiously hoped secession would soon dissolve of its own accord. Many Northerners recognized the economic significance of the South, fearing secession more than they loathed slavery, but Lincoln insisted that the Union would not fire the first shot.

On April 12, 1861, Davis ordered his forces to fire at Northern-controlled Fort Sumter in Charleston, South Carolina. Lincoln responded by sending 75,000 troops into the South. Within weeks, Virginia, North Carolina, Tennessee, and Arkansas joined the Confederacy, making a total of eleven states. The Civil War had begun.

GENERAL ROBERT E. LEE
1861–65

From the outset, the Confederate Army representing the Southern states was vastly outnumbered by the Union forces in the North. But size was not to be the only factor determining military victories in the Civil War: Conflicting loyalties also played a major role.

A week after the bombardment of Fort Sumter, Lincoln appointed Robert E. Lee as commander of the Union forces. An experienced and well-respected colonel in the US Army, Lee had already proven his talent for tactical warfare. But he was also a Virginian, and Virginia's ensuing secession from the Union forced him to reject the commission and defect to the Confederate Army, unable and unwilling to lead the Union into battle against his home state. Other commanders and troops did likewise, and the Union was forced to fill its vacancies with new leaders and inexperienced conscripts rather than military veterans.

In the first year of the war, General Lee acted as a key military adviser to the Confederate leaders, as a result of which he was given command of the Confederate Army in June 1862. He was adept at both leading and confronting an army on the field, and many historians agree that he was one of the last great eighteenth-century-style generals. Despite facing a more modern style of total warfare, in which little distinction was made between civilian and military targets, General Lee distinguished himself during the Civil War, and was promoted to general in chief just months before the Confederate Army was finally forced into surrender.

THE FIRST BATTLE OF BULL RUN
July 21, 1861

Civil War began in earnest with the First Battle of Bull Run, in Virginia, on July 21, 1861. This first major clash between the Confederate and the Union armies proved to both sides that the Civil War would be a bitter and lengthy engagement, a far cry from the notion of one glorious, decisive victory that had previously held sway in the North.

The Union Army assembled in four divisions, under the command of Brigadier General Irvin McDowell. There were two Confederate armies: General Beauregard's Confederate Army of the Potomac, and General Joseph E. Johnston's Army of the Shenandoah. The Confederate leaders were better strategists and outmaneuvered the Union forces. A final advance of Beauregard's men forced the Union soldiers into a chaotic retreat. But the human cost of Bull Run was a grim warning of what lay ahead: New weaponry felled vast numbers, totaling more than 5,000 dead, missing, or injured, far outstripping anything the US Army had suffered in a single battle before.

After Bull Run, there were military changes on both sides. The Confederate Army of the Potomac merged with the Army of the Shenandoah to form the Army of Northern Virginia, commanded by General Joseph E. Johnston. Bull Run strengthened Lincoln's resolve to find effective military leadership, and he gave chief command of the Union forces over to the skilled but cautious General George McClellan. Lincoln regretted this appointment when McClellan proved less aggressive in battle than he had hoped, and replaced McClellan with Henry W. Halleck in March 1862, although McClellan remained major general of the Union's Army of the Potomac.

GENERALS ULYSSES S. GRANT AND WILLIAM SHERMAN
1864–65

The Confederate Army had the early advantage of proven military leaders where the Union had few, but that balance soon changed. Many higher-ranking Confederates died early in the war, but as it entered its decisive stages, two considerable Union generals emerged.

Ulysses S. Grant had an unremarkable early army career, graduating from West Point in 1843 and fighting in the Mexican-American War. In 1854, unfulfilled by a peacetime army life, he resigned and embarked upon fruitless ventures in farming and bill collecting. When the Civil War began, the governor of Illinois gave him command over a challenging regiment of volunteers, a job he embraced with daring and logic, quickly earning him a series of promotions.

Grant was a calm, disciplined, and strategic leader. In March 1864, Lincoln promoted him to commander in chief of the US Army, remarking, "As soon as I put a man in command of the army, they all wanted me to be the general. Now it isn't so with Grant. He hasn't told me what his plans are. I don't know and I don't want to know. I am glad to find a man who can go ahead without me."

Grant's promotion handed control of Union forces in the West to General William Sherman, who had fought under Grant in a series of decisive battles. In contrast to Confederate General Robert E. Lee, Sherman was a thoroughly modern military strategist who embraced the new form of total warfare, albeit ruthlessly on occasion. He was rewarded for his dedication by being promoted to the head of the US Army when General Grant became president in 1868.

THE BATTLE OF SHILOH
April 1862

arly in 1862, Union forces led by Ulysses S. Grant launched an offensive in the Mississippi Valley and took control of Nashville, Tennessee. Grant's troops then camped at the Pittsburg Landing in Tennessee, awaiting reinforcements. His plan was to launch an assault on the Memphis and Charleston Railroad in order to destroy the Confederacy's only reliable supply route between the Mississippi Valley and the East Coast. But the Confederate commander, General Albert Johnston, planned a preemptive strike before Union reinforcements arrived: On April 6, 1862, 50,000 Confederate troops advanced on unguarded Union camps at Shiloh on the Pittsburg Landing, taking them entirely by surprise.

During the first day of the battle, Confederate forces gained ground but suffered the loss of General Johnston. By nightfall, Union reinforcements had finally arrived. In a decisive counteroffensive the following day, General Grant overwhelmed the exhausted Confederate Army, pushing Beauregard into retreat. The staggering human losses far exceeded Bull Run: 23,746 casualties in two days.

New Orleans, Natchez, and Memphis gradually fell to the Union in the early summer of 1862. In June, the tide began to turn: General Lee halted Union troops advancing on Richmond, Virginia, and went on to force a Union retreat back to Washington, D.C., at the Second Battle of Bull Run in August. By the late summer of 1862, it seemed the Union was on the run and Confederate forces were no longer on the defensive.

THE BATTLE OF ANTIETAM
September 1862

As August eased into September, General Lee planned his first Confederate push into Union territory. He chose to advance first into Maryland, a slave state he hoped to lure to the Confederacy, and an agricultural state whose crops he hoped would feed his armies through the winter. From there he intended to march on Washington, DC, and persuade the United Kingdom and France to recognize the Confederacy, despite Queen Victoria's assertion of British neutrality. It was an ambitious plan, but Lee, capitalizing on a run of victories, was optimistic.

His tired, ragged, and hungry army advanced into Maryland, 5,000 of them crossing the Potomac River and camping on the outskirts of Frederick, and 40,000 more following. The day after Lee and his men moved northwest, a Union corps camped in the same field and discovered a discarded envelope containing three cigars wrapped in a piece of paper on which Lee's planned four-pronged attack on Maryland and Pennsylvania was detailed. General McClellan was now able to anticipate Lee's advance.

McClellan's army met Lee's at the Battle of Antietam, in Maryland, on September 17. Although his soldiers outnumbered Lee's two to one, McClellan did not send all of his men, and the battle was not conclusive. But it was the bloodiest yet, with bodies scattered three deep across the battlefield: 4,300 died and 18,000 were wounded in a single day. Lee retreated across the Potomac to Virginia, leaving the Union with a strategic victory.

THE EMANCIPATION PROCLAMATION
1862

At the outset of war, President Lincoln's primary concern had been to keep the border slave states of Maryland, Delaware, Kentucky, and Missouri in the Union. To that end, Congress had passed the Crittenden Compromise, offering assurance that the Union had no plans for abolition. But when an influx of fugitive slaves joined the ranks of the Union Army, the question of slavery became impossible to ignore. Furthermore, their knowledge of Confederate movements in the South provided an invaluable source of intelligence that Union leaders couldn't afford to dismiss.

Suddenly the anti-slavery lobby was able to use emancipation as a war cry. Slave labor was the cornerstone of the Southern economy, and to outlaw it—as the government technically could, since it refused to recognize the independence of the Confederate States— would seriously undermine the Southern war effort. Emancipation was no longer a liberal aspiration but a Unionist demand.

Bolstered by military success in Maryland, a crucial border slave state, Lincoln signed the Emancipation Proclamation on September 22, 1862. The Proclamation outlawed slave ownership in any Confederate state that failed to rejoin the Union by January 1, 1863, although Unionist border slave states were exempt. But Lincoln had not counted on the adverse effect it would have among working-class Northerners, whose support for the Civil War diminished amid fears that an influx of African American laborers would threaten their job security. The number of volunteers consequently fell so sharply that the Union had to resort to conscription in March 1863. That same spring, African Americans were recruited for the first black regiments of the US Army.

THE BATTLE OF GETTYSBURG
July 1863

In May 1863, the Confederates defeated Union forces at Chancellorsville, Virginia, but lost at Jackson, Mississippi, and were besieged by General Grant's forces at Vicksburg. In June, the Confederate general Lee embarked upon another campaign to push through to Washington, D.C., by advancing into Pennsylvania toward Gettysburg.

On July 1, 1863, the Battle of Gettysburg began. It was a ferocious three-day conflict involving a total of 165,000 men, the largest battle ever to be fought on American soil. The Union put up a strong defense, digging trenches and resisting wave after wave of Confederate attacks. On the third day, Confederate leaders made a final concentrated advance of more than 10,000 men toward the center of the Union line. Almost half the advancing Confederates were mowed down by Union artillery fire as they crossed the open field.

Those three days resulted in more than 50,000 casualties. Lee ordered a retreat and Confederate troops fled the North; the decimated and battle-weary Union forces made no attempt at pursuit.

Gettysburg was a major turning point in the war: The Confederates lost a third of their total army and, as Lee began his retreat, Vicksburg capitulated to Grant's siege. This devastating surrender of 30,000 Confederate troops put the Mississippi Valley under Union control, leading many people to believe that the end of the Civil War was in sight.

THE GETTYSBURG ADDRESS
November 19, 1863

On November 19, 1863, President Lincoln gave his finest speech at the dedication of a military cemetery at Gettysburg, the site of the Civil War's most ferocious battle.

"Fourscore and seven years ago, our fathers brought forth on this continent a new nation, conceived in liberty and dedicated to the proposition that all men are created equal. Now we are engaged in a great civil war, testing whether that nation or any nation so conceived and so dedicated can long endure. We are met on a great battlefield of that war. We have come to dedicate a portion of that field as a final resting-place for those who here gave their lives that that nation might live. It is altogether fitting and proper that we should do this. But in a larger sense, we cannot dedicate, we cannot consecrate, we cannot hallow this ground. The brave men, living and dead, who struggled here have consecrated it far above our poor power to add or detract. The world will little note nor long remember what we say here, but it can never forget what they did here. It is for us the living rather to be dedicated here to the unfinished work which they who fought here have thus far so nobly advanced. It is rather for us to be here dedicated to the great task remaining before us—that from these honored dead we take increased devotion to that cause for which they gave the last full measure of devotion—that we here highly resolve that these dead shall not have died in vain, that this nation under God shall have a new birth of freedom, and that government of the people, by the people, for the people shall not perish from the earth."

SHERMAN'S MARCH TO THE SEA
November 1864

By the end of 1863, the Union position had grown stronger in the South, despite defeat by the Confederates at Chickamauga in September. General Grant's control over the Mississippi Valley meant that the Union had effectively divided the Confederacy in two, separating east from west. By November 1863, Grant had further weakened the South by taking Tennessee, putting his troops in prime position to march across the South to the sea.

This new assault was led by General Sherman. Grant had ordered him to march on Atlanta with a force of 60,000 men; they took the city in September and their march toward Savannah began in mid-November. As they left Atlanta, Sherman ordered the evacuation and burning of the city. He continued to pursue this scorched-earth policy as he advanced through Georgia, leaving behind him a forty-mile-wide scar of destroyed railroads, bridges, towns, and anything else with the potential to bolster the Confederate cause.

General Beauregard was dispatched to halt Sherman's advance, although nobody in the Confederate camp was entirely sure of his final destination. Orders were given for Confederate civilians and slaves to evacuate farms, and to help destroy roads and bridges lying in the Union's path. By now, however, the people of Georgia were disillusioned by the war and few took up the call. Just before Christmas of 1864, Sherman marched into Savannah unopposed, leaving the Confederacy divided north from south and east from west.

SURRENDER AT APPOMATTOX
April 9, 1865

With Georgia under Union control, General Sherman led a similarly destructive assault upon first South Carolina and then North Carolina in the early months of 1865. In his wake, slaves rose up against their owners, just as Congress approved the Thirteenth Amendment abolishing slavery throughout the Union, with no exceptions for border states. Lincoln was elected president for a second term, and pledged to "bind up the nation's wounds."

In June 1864, Generals Grant and Lee both marched on the town of Petersburg, Virginia, which controlled the railroad into the Confederate capital, Richmond. Confederate forces arrived first, so Grant embarked upon a siege of the city that was to last nine months. General Lee had seen Grant's siege tactics work with devastating effect at Vicksburg the previous summer, but his need to protect Richmond left him little choice.

Daily shellfire and intense hunger took its toll, and Lee's men began to desert. On April 2, 1865, Grant drove the Confederates out of Petersburg, and Richmond fell the following day. Lee and his considerably depleted army fled the city but were easily apprehended, and he surrendered to the Union at the Appomattox Court House in Virginia on April 9.

President Lincoln insisted upon generous treatment of the surrendering Confederate forces, echoing the speech he had made at his second inauguration, in which he called for "malice toward none" and "charity for all." The Civil War, in which over 600,000 men died either in action or from their injuries, was finally over.

THE ASSASSINATION OF LINCOLN
April 14, 1865

John Wilkes Booth was an actor from Maryland with strong Confederate sympathies. In 1864, Booth and eight others plotted to kidnap President Lincoln and hold him hostage until the federal government released Confederate prisoners of war. But their plans were foiled by a late change in Lincoln's schedule.

In early April 1865, General Lee's surrender and Lincoln's speech calling for African Americans to be granted the right to vote prompted Booth to renew his scheme. Vehemently opposed to African American suffrage and determined the war was not over, Booth and his fellow conspirators now planned a series of assassinations: President Lincoln and General Grant would be killed at Washington's Ford's Theatre on April 14. Vice President Andrew Johnson and Secretary of State William Seward would be killed that same evening.

General Grant escaped his fate through a last-minute change of plans, but Booth made his way to the theater's Presidential Box and shot Lincoln in the back of the head before leaping onto the stage and absconding through the wings. Lincoln died the following morning. Seward survived a savage knife attack in his bed that evening, while Johnson was spared by the failed nerve of his would-be assassin, George Atzerodt, who instead sat drinking in the bar at the hotel in which the vice president was staying, before disappearing.

Booth was later tracked down in Maryland and killed by Union soldiers. All eight conspirators, including Atzerodt, were arrested and tried by military tribunal, and all were found guilty; four were hanged.

RECONSTRUCTION
AND
INDUSTRIALIZATION

THE HOMESTEAD ACT
1863

The Civil War brought about a dramatic transformation of the American economy, as the storekeepers and farmers who had previously typified the Northern states made way for industrialization on a grand scale. The prewar secession of eleven Southern states also gave Northern Congressmen the chance to pursue policies they had long wanted to implement.

For several years, Congress had hotly debated a Republican-backed plan to give free land to settlers in the West. But Southern Congressmen had thrown it out at every opportunity, fearing that a rise in the number of small farms would threaten large plantations. Southern secession gave the Republican Party the chance it needed, and the Homestead Act came into effect on January 1, 1863, the same day as the Emancipation Proclamation.

The Homestead Act offered the opportunity for settlers to claim 160 acres of publicly owned land in exchange for a nominal fee, on the condition that they remain resident on the land for the first five years.

Homesteads were particularly attractive to new immigrants and to the sons of previously established farmers. By the early twentieth century, the act had enabled over 600,000 families to claim farms of their own. Its honorable, small-scale intentions became outdated as the number of agricultural corporations increased, however, and it was eventually repealed in 1976.

ANDREW JOHNSON AND
RECONSTRUCTION
1866–77

After Lincoln's death, Vice President Andrew Johnson took over the remainder of his term. Johnson had entered Tennessee politics as a pro-slavery Democrat, but with a deep-seated mistrust of plantation owners. After Tennessee's secession, Johnson was the only Southern senator to remain in Congress, where his "unwavering commitment to the Union" impressed Lincoln.

Johnson's plans for Reconstruction focused on the interests of working-class white Southerners. He implemented Lincoln's amnesty for any Confederate who pledged allegiance to the Union, and ignored radical Republican cries for harsher punishment. But he excluded plantation owners, whom he blamed for the war, insisting they beg in person for a presidential pardon. Finally, he allowed any state that adopted the Thirteenth Amendment, abolishing slavery, back into the Union before passing control of the plantations back to former slave owners and declaring Reconstruction complete.

Steadily, the former Confederate states rejoined the Union but retaliated against the Thirteenth Amendment with Black Codes, depriving freed slaves of the rights to vote, own property, testify against whites, or bear arms. In 1866, Congress counteracted with the Civil Rights Act, denying states the power to restrict African American voting rights. Johnson tried to veto the act, but the Republicans pushed it through and subsequently adopted the Fourteenth Amendment, making the protection of the rights of all Americans a government responsibility. As Reconstruction deepened the divide between Johnson and the Republicans, the states were also still far from united.

THE IMPEACHMENT OF ANDREW JOHNSON
1868

A Republican Congressional victory in 1866 left Johnson powerless to prevent the Republicans' radical Reconstruction Act from being passed. The divide between the political parties had never been greater, and Congress's quarrel with the president was about to take a dramatic turn.

In 1867, the Republican majority in Congress passed the Tenure of Office Act, prohibiting a presidential dismissal of a Senate-appointed official. Johnson declared the act unconstitutional and dismissed Edwin Stanton, war secretary and radical Republican sympathizer. In response, citing Article II, Section 4 of the Constitution, Congress began impeachment proceedings against Johnson for "high crimes and misdemeanors."

Although it passed easily through the House of Representatives, the impeachment still had to be ratified by the Senate. This was no sure thing. First, Johnson had no vice president and his potential successor under succession laws of the time was the unpopular radical president pro tempore of the Senate, Benjamin Wade. Secondly, Johnson's lawyers had been working hard convincing Republican senators that, if reinstated, the president would no longer oppose Reconstruction. The final vote in May 1868 fell just short of upholding the impeachment, and Johnson remained in power.

Days later, Ulysses S. Grant was nominated the Republican presidential candidate for the election of 1868. Johnson, whose controversial presidency had lost him a great deal of party support, lost the Democratic nomination to Horatio Seymour. Grant was elected president and took the oath of office in March 1869.

THE GILDED AGE
1870–90

In 1873, Mark Twain co-authored a satirical novel that was to launch his literary career and lend its title to the era. *The Gilded Age: A Tale of Today* was a witty attack on the corruption, greed, and dishonesty that characterized the post-Civil War period.

The second half of the nineteenth century was a time of glittering progress, invention, and prosperity. A population boom raised demand for advancements in fuel and food supply, building materials, and transport, and both coal mining and steel production witnessed a significant increase in output. Meanwhile, the new transcontinental railroads stretched from coast to coast, introducing new areas to commercial farming and uniting the vast nation under the umbrella of supply and demand, and striking skyscrapers began to emerge across American cities.

But this rapid industrialization was, in part, achieved at the expense of the poor and powerless. As railroads expanded across Native American lands, the economic boom widened the gap between rich and poor, leaving vast sections of the working class below the poverty line while their employers enjoyed unprecedented prosperity. During the same period, newly granted civil liberties fueled the rise of white supremacists and the Ku Klux Klan, forcing many African Americans to flee their homes in the South.

By the time the Gilded Age ended, however, the United States had undeniably experienced a period of record economic progress, and was fast becoming one of the world's wealthiest countries.

THE AGE OF INVENTION
1850–90

The Gilded Age saw commercial inventions become big business. Funded by Western Union to develop his ideas and patents into practical technologies for the modern era, Thomas Edison, the greatest inventor of his day, developed the phonograph, the lightbulb, and motion pictures, as well as improving upon Alexander Graham Bell's telephone in the late 1870s.

Edison's lightbulb, patented in 1880, came at the pinnacle of an international race to secure electricity patents. With the public gradually accepting that the volatile commodity could be harnessed for home use, Edison and his nearest rival, entrepreneur George Westinghouse, engaged in a "War of Currents" to determine who would control the mass generation of commercial electricity. In 1882, Edison established the world's first distribution system in Manhattan, serving a small number of local consumers, although Westinghouse soon developed a transformer that enabled electric power to be generated long distances away from the areas it supplied.

In architecture, the innovative use of iron skeletons to support building structures led to skyscrapers dominating urban skylines. The first example was by William LeBaron Jenney, whose Home Insurance Building in Chicago was erected in 1885. But vast multistory buildings were made viable only for living and working space by the inventions of others, in particular Elisha Otis's hydraulic elevator—in use to this day—and William Baldwin's domestic radiator.

A staggering half a million patents were issued during the thirty years of the Gilded Age. Some, such as the transatlantic cable, had an instant impact. Others, such as Edison's moving-picture camera, only achieved significant commercial recognition years later.

INDUSTRIALIZATION AND THE RISE OF THE INDUSTRIAL TYCOON
1865–1900

After the Civil War, the United States experienced a period of rapid industrialization and urbanization. The cities around the Great Lakes came to form an industrial heartland, with Pittsburgh at its center, as its iron and steel industry emerged as the world leader by the end of the nineteenth century.

Coal, another vital resource, stoked the furnace for industrial growth. Only twenty states had mines before the Civil War, but growing railroad networks enabled previously inaccessible coalfields to be opened up. By the end of the century, coal mining was big business, with a handful of large firms dominating the industry.

Meanwhile, Edwin Drake's method of sinking pipelines into bedrock made commercial oil drilling possible by the 1860s. An insightful businessman from Ohio capitalized on this industry's early disorganization. Publicly stating that he believed oil had "no future," John D. Rockefeller began secretly buying up oil companies and arranging lucrative rail transport deals to give him a price advantage over his competitors. Within seven years, his sidestepping of American antimonopoly laws gave Rockefeller's Standard Oil control of more than 90 percent of the American oil business, ultimately making him the world's first billionaire.

Other tycoons grew rich on the profits of industrialization, although many were also keen philanthropists. One such man was Daniel Guggenheim, a second-generation Swiss immigrant from Philadelphia whose father wisely invested in two Colorado lead and silver mines in the 1880s. Daniel's shrewd management of his father's mines expanded the company and made him a powerful multimillionaire.

ANDREW CARNEGIE AND JOHN PIERPONT MORGAN, SR.
1835–1919 and 1837–1913

A ndrew Carnegie and John Pierpont Morgan, Sr., epitomized the super-rich tycoons at the economic heart of the Gilded Age. Both were hardworking, gifted businessmen who donated extensively to charity—Carnegie funded America's first public libraries—but at the same time opposed workplace unions and monopolized major industries.

Carnegie was a first-generation immigrant from Scotland, a cotton factory employee who, thanks to the Civil War, had worked his way up to senior management positions on the Pennsylvania railroads before moving into oil and then steel. Importing a state-of-the-art production method, Carnegie became market leader, with a stake in every stage of the steel production process. By the 1890s, he was working toward the monopoly of the industry and had amassed a considerable fortune.

An opportune meeting at a party with banking tycoon John Pierpont Morgan, Sr., (J. P. Morgan) provided Carnegie with the backing he needed to form the multimillion-dollar corporation US Steel. Morgan came from a banking family and had spent the Civil War financing a profitable trade in arms. After the war, Morgan's vastly successful bank focused on monopolizing the railroads.

Morgan and Carnegie's joint venture dominated the American steel industry at a time when demand for steel was increasing rapidly. By the turn of the century, the United States was the international market leader in steel, a position that was reinforced as countries industrialized and armed themselves in the buildup to World War One.

TRANSCONTINENTAL RAILROADS AND THE ROBBER BARONS
1869–90

After Reconstruction, the desire to populate the West acted as an industrial catalyst, and the thriving American steel industry supplied the raw materials for an astonishing expansion of the railroad network.

For some individuals, christened "robber barons" by historian Charles Francis Adams in 1878, the railroads were a ticket to enormous wealth. Leland Stanford and Cornelius Vanderbilt (who founded the universities of the same names) were among those who grew rich through their shrewd management of railroad construction companies. Congressman Oakes Ames, a director of the Union Pacific Railroad, epitomized the lengths to which some entrepreneurs went to curry political favor for their ventures, creating a company to manage the railroad's finances, and then offering half-price shares in it to prominent men in Washington, D.C.

Nevertheless, by 1890, five railroads crossed the continent, and the social and geographical landscape of the United States had changed forever. The railroads enabled raw materials and manufactured goods to be transported on a vast scale, while brands became recognizable nationwide and chain stores sprouted up across the country. Popular mobility became a real possibility for the first time, and the railroad companies even instigated the creation of four time zones in order to facilitate this; before 1883, time was kept according to the position of the sun, making it impossible to establish standard timetables. Perhaps most significantly, with coast-to-coast journeys now taking days rather than months, reaching and populating the untamed West no longer presented a life-endangering mission.

CUSTER'S LAST STAND
June 1876

B y the 1860s, Native Americans had been pushed into
the heart of the country. But after Reconstruction,
their presence on unsettled territory presented an
increasing problem for railroad companies, expansionist
politicians, and cattlemen fighting for control of land. Territorial
disputes frequently descended into armed violence between Native
Americans and the US Army, but this escalated after a Dakota Sioux
uprising led to a month of bloody fighting in 1862. Similar battles
were waged across the Great Plains for the next thirty years.

In 1874, General George Armstrong Custer was sent into the
Black Hills, South Dakota, to chart the area and investigate gold-
mining potential. His much-publicized discovery of gold prompted
a rush of prospectors into Native American sacred lands, resulting in
increased hostility with the Sioux, and ultimately the Great Sioux
War of 1876–77.

The war's most notorious encounter was the Battle of the Little
Bighorn. On June 25, 1876, Custer led a 650-strong regiment through
South Dakota gold fields and confronted 4,000 Cheyenne and Sioux
warriors led by Sitting Bull and Crazy Horse, who had congregated
along the Bighorn River. Underestimating the number of warriors
and acting against orders, Custer divided his regiment and ordered
an attack, in which he and over 250 of his men were killed.

The press glorified Custer's "Last Stand," and the battle proved
a hollow victory for the Native Americans, whose resistance to the
United States was growing increasingly futile. The army forced the
Sioux into reservations and killed Crazy Horse when he resisted
capture.

TAMING THE WILD WEST
1867–87

The Wild West has long been the stuff of Hollywood legend: heroic sheriffs, untamable outlaws, and free-spirited cowboys living on the open range. The legacy of this period still permeates popular culture, even though, in reality, the era of the large-scale, cross-country cattle drive lasted only from 1867, when the first cattle-shipping railhead was established in Abilene, Kansas, until the early 1890s, by which time railroads formed an efficient cargo network across the United States.

Cowboys were low-paid workers who drove thousands of Texan longhorns north to the Kansas Pacific railroad stations in Missouri and Kansas: Kansas City, Sedalia, Dodge City, Cheyenne, Wichita, and Abilene, which gained an especially lawless and decadent reputation thanks to its location at the center of the lucrative trade. Although shoot-outs were rare, these Western settlements needed policing, and men such as notorious gunfighter "Wild Bill" Hickok were soon brought in as marshals. Hickok only shot two men during his spell in Abilene, but along with fellow marshal Wyatt Earp and outlaws Jesse James and Billy the Kid, he gained iconic status when his exploits were glorified by reporters in the East.

Although cattle ranches exist to this day, long-distance cattle drives had become a thing of the past by the end of the century, as cattle were grazed on vast areas of the Northern plains, enclosed by barbed wire. Oil, lumber, and natural mineral mining transformed the West's economy and vast numbers of the rural population steadily migrated to expanding cities such as Los Angeles and San Francisco.

IMMIGRATION AND THE MAKING OF MODERN AMERICA
1829–1924

The rich ethnic diversity of modern urban America has its roots in the late nineteenth century. Over 5 million people, mostly Irish, Germans, and Italians, arrived in the 1880s alone. By 1910, over 40 percent of New Yorkers were first-generation immigrants, and other industrial cities such as Boston and Minneapolis experienced a similar influx. The boom in industrial development during this period created thousands of jobs in manual labor, which were largely filled by immigrants; railroad construction, for instance, was dominated by Chinese and Irish workers.

The "huddled masses yearning to breathe free," as described in a contemporary poem by Emma Lazarus, sailed past the Statue of Liberty—erected in 1886—into New York Harbor, having first to endure the rigors of Ellis Island. Established in 1892, the Ellis Island Immigration Bureau screened arrivals for anyone likely to be a danger or burden to the state, but only around 2 percent were ever rejected and sent home. By the time Ellis Island closed in 1954, over 12 million immigrants had passed through.

The rise in cheap labor prompted initial unease in the larger cities, and coincided with a period of increased patriotism; the daily Pledge of Allegiance originated around this time. Nevertheless, cultures from across the world gradually merged, and the coexistence of patriotism and ethnic diversity helped to shape modern-day America—a nation itself established by immigrants seeking liberty.

THE RISE OF THE UNIONS
1880–1932

The concentrated wealth and great political influence of late-nineteenth-century tycoons did much to restrict the growth of industrial unions—organizations that monitored and promoted the fair treatment and payment of workers, and which were becoming more prominent in industrialized countries. Moreover, ethnic diversity among America's new immigrant workforce led to clashes between Italian and Irish, Irish and German, and European and Chinese workers, and made cooperation seem unachievable.

In the 1880s, a union called "The Noble and Holy Order of the Knights of Labor" marked a new era of organized labor. The Knights argued that poor working conditions amounted to a loss of economic freedom comparable to slavery, and demanded economic liberty for all by way of broad and idealistic political reform. Early successes boosted their membership, but a bomb attack on Chicago police during a Knights' strike in 1886 earned the movement an anarchic reputation, and support fell away.

The American Federation of Labor—the AFL—founded by New York cigar maker Daniel Gompers in 1886, was more successful. Gompers rejected the broad idealism of the Knights of Labor, disagreeing that unions should become politically active. He gained support from all sides of the political divide, although union membership was restricted to "skilled workers," which effectively excluded a large percentage of the African American workforce. Gompers engaged only in direct negotiation with employers, looking to achieve very specific ends, such as an eight-hour day. He effectively depoliticized unionism, an approach known as "business unionism," and contributed to the union movement's rise to respectability.

THE SHERMAN ANTITRUST ACT
1890

The bankers and businessmen who financed the transcontinental railroads with their corrupt ways and ruthless monopolizing were both wealthy and powerful. However, by the end of the 1880s, the railroad practices they influenced had become unpopular: High prices, low wages, and an uncompromising response to unionizing prompted an increasing clamor for reform.

The government response was weak: By this time, too many politicians had been corrupted by the tycoons' *de facto* control over federal purse strings. President Grover Cleveland established the Interstate Commerce Commission in 1887 in an attempt to oversee the setting of fair, standardized rates for the transportation of agricultural and commercial goods. The ICC had very limited economic power, and the results were unimpressive.

In 1890, Cleveland's successor, President Benjamin Harrison, responded to continued pressure with the Sherman Antitrust Act. The Sherman Act—named after its author, Senator John Sherman—was the first federal law to set out legal restrictions against monopolies. It made attempted or actual monopolization of any sector of national or international commerce illegal, and made a felon of anyone who conspired to suppress fair competition for his own personal gain.

The Sherman Antitrust Act is noteworthy as the first of a series of increasingly refined antitrust laws in the United States. In the years following its ratification, the act was used by Presidents Theodore Roosevelt and William H. Taft to force the breaking up of some of America's most dominant monopolies: the Northern Securities Company in 1904, Standard Oil in 1909, and the American Tobacco Company in 1911.

"Remember the *Maine*!"
The Spanish-American War
1898

As the European superpowers of the late nineteenth century flexed their imperial muscles in Africa and Asia, a growing body of Americans clamored for American expansion. Industrial giants, bankers, political thinkers, and even missionaries argued that overseas expansion was America's "Manifest Destiny." Within the government, expansionists including Theodore Roosevelt felt that a foreign war would help the United States make its mark on the world.

Public pressure for war intensified when rival newspaper giants Joseph Pulitzer and William Randolph Hearst whipped up a pro-war frenzy with their wildly exaggerated reports of Spanish atrocities against Cubans fighting for independence. With the Monroe Doctrine in mind, President William McKinley sent the USS *Maine* to Havana Harbor in January 1898, to guard American interests in Cuba. The battleship sank in an explosion on February 15, thought at the time to be caused by a Spanish mine, resulting in the deaths of 274 Americans. The sensationalist newspapers ran with the battle cry "Remember the *Maine*! To hell with Spain!"

McKinley feared his war-hungry party would fragment if he pursued a diplomatic resolution. War, when it came, was swift and decisive, quickly escalating into an imperialistic attack on Spanish colonies, including Cuba, Wake Island, the Philippines, Puerto Rico, and Guam. Spain surrendered after three months, leaving the United States with the makings of a Pacific empire, of which Puerto Rico and Guam remain United States territories. By the end of 1898, with the further annexation of the future state of Hawaii, the United States had secured its place on the international stage.

BLACK AMERICA: "SEPARATE BUT EQUAL"
1890–1909

Although the Fifteenth Amendment of 1870 had made voting a constitutional right regardless of color, the introduction of literacy and poll-tax restrictions by every Southern state between 1890 and 1906 effectively disenfranchised African Americans. While their social and economic status remained intolerable, there was also the new terror of lynching by the Ku Klux Klan and other mobs. A study at the Tuskegee Institute in Alabama indicated that almost 3,500 African Americans were lynched between 1882 and 1968.

Some dared to fight back. In 1896, Howard Plessy refused to give up his seat in a whites-only section of a New Orleans train. *Plessy v. Ferguson* went to the Supreme Court, which ruled that segregation was constitutional if provision was "separate but equal." This prompted a rash of Southern segregation laws, known as "Jim Crow laws" after the 1820s minstrel character. Extending to every public facility from schools to cemeteries, the "separate but equal" ruling was seldom practiced: Facilities for black and white people were rarely equal.

Other African American leaders campaigned hard for equal rights. Former slave Booker T. Washington urged African Americans to stop anti-segregation agitation and focus instead on economic advancement. W. E. B. Du Bois, the first black person to receive a Harvard Ph.D., rejected Washington's conservatism and co-founded the National Association for the Advancement of Colored People (NAACP) in 1909. Its mission was clear: to "advance the interest of colored citizens," and to secure for them impartial suffrage, justice, education, and employment. It was the first step in a growing civil rights movement that later dominated the 1960s.

SUSAN B. ANTHONY
February 15, 1820–March 13, 1906

Susan Brownell Anthony was born into a family of Massachusetts Quakers who relocated to New York in 1826. In 1839, after finishing her education at a Philadelphia boarding school, she began teaching in order to help her family financially. In 1846, she was promoted to headmistress at Canajoharie Academy in upstate New York. Women teachers were paid a fraction of what their male colleagues earned, an injustice that inspired Susan to campaign for equal pay later in life.

After giving up teaching in 1848, Anthony moved back to Rochester, New York, where she began campaigning on behalf of women suffering abuse at the hands of alcoholic husbands; she became secretary for the Daughters of Temperance and delivered her first public speech in 1849.

In 1851, a chance meeting in Seneca Falls, New York, brought Anthony into contact with women's rights activist Elizabeth Cady Stanton, and led to a lifelong friendship and working partnership. In September 1852, Anthony attended the women's rights convention in Syracuse and became convinced that "the right women needed above every other . . . was the right of suffrage." She dedicated her life to the cause and began to emerge as a compelling new voice.

Anthony and Stanton co-founded the National Woman Suffrage Association (later the National American Woman Suffrage Association). Between 1868 and 1872, Anthony published a weekly journal, *The Revolution*, through which she campaigned for federal voting reform. Although she did not live to see American women granted the right to vote in federal elections, it was due to her dedication and unwavering beliefs that they eventually did.

THE STRUGGLE FOR EQUALITY
1848–1920

American women's struggle for equality rose out of the pre–Civil War temperance and anti-slavery movements. In 1840, Quakers Elizabeth Cady Stanton and Lucretia Mott attended the World Anti-Slavery Convention in London and were outraged at being excluded as delegates on account of their gender. In July 1848, they organized the first official Women's Rights Convention at Seneca Falls, New York. Stanton scripted the Declaration of Sentiments, stating: "We hold these truths to be self evident: that all men and women are created equal."

In 1866, Stanton, Mott, and Susan B. Anthony joined with black rights activists to form the American Equal Rights Association, to promote the cause of sexual and racial equality. When the Fourteenth and Fifteenth Amendments gave the vote to African American men but ignored the rights of women, Stanton and Anthony broke away and set up the National Woman Suffrage Association, which later merged with the American Woman Suffrage Association, founded by prominent activist Lucy Stone, to campaign for the vote.

Following decades of struggle and vigorous campaigning, individual states bowed to overwhelming pressure and, in 1890, began to grant women the right to vote in nonfederal elections. President Wilson effectively joined the cause in 1918, proclaiming that women's suffrage was vital as a morale-boosting "war measure." After a long and hard-won battle in Congress, the Nineteenth Amendment was passed on June 4, 1919, and ratified on August 18, 1920: "The right of citizens of the United States to vote shall not be denied or abridged by the United States or by any State on account of sex."

THEODORE ROOSEVELT
October 27, 1858–January 6, 1919

Theodore Roosevelt was born into a wealthy New York banking family. He graduated from Harvard in 1880, subsequently abandoning Columbia Law School to serve on the New York State Assembly. In 1884, following the death of his wife Alice, he left the city to become a cowboy and cattle rancher in the Dakota Territory.

Having remodeled himself as a Republican politician, Roosevelt was appointed assistant secretary of the Navy in 1897. The following year, he returned a hero from the Spanish-American War and was elected governor of New York. His Progressive policies made the Republicans increasingly uneasy, and he was appointed McKinley's vice president in an attempt to contain his influence. When McKinley was assassinated in September 1901, however, forty-two-year-old Roosevelt became the youngest president to date.

Under Roosevelt, the United States became a world power for the first time. He oversaw the construction of the Panama Canal, curbed the widespread abuse of power among industrial giants, and was the first president to take a stance on long-term environmental conservation. An unsuccessful assassination attempt left him with a bullet in his chest, but didn't limit his energy.

Having declined a third term in 1908, Roosevelt formed the short-lived Bull Moose Party when his successor and rival, William H. Taft, was nominated by the Republicans in 1912. He drew numerous liberal Republicans away from Taft, but in doing so handed victory to Democrat Woodrow Wilson and left the Republican Party in the hands of conservatives.

Roosevelt died in New York in 1919, and is immortalized alongside Washington, Jefferson, and Lincoln on Mount Rushmore.

THE MUCKRAKERS
1900–06

Roosevelt's Progressivism was symptomatic of the era. The Gilded Age had left an intolerable legacy of corruption and greed in the United States, one mirrored in industrialized countries around the world. A new breed of journalists declared war on the fraud and dishonesty rife in business and politics, and on the shocking conditions to which America's disadvantaged were subjected. Leading activists included journalist Ida Tarbell, who published a damning exposé of Standard Oil in 1904, and novelist Lincoln Steffens, who attacked the corrupt relationship between party bosses and the heads of industry in *The Shame of the Cities* that same year.

The bleak social pessimism of this journalistic trend irritated Roosevelt and prompted him to label its proponents "Muckrakers" in 1906, a reference to an unsavory character in John Bunyan's *Pilgrim's Progress*. Roosevelt nonetheless faced the abuses they highlighted squarely, acknowledging that "There are, in the body politic . . . many and grave evils, and there is urgent necessity for the sternest war upon them."

Most famous among the Muckrakers was the novelist Upton Sinclair, whose exposé of Chicago slaughterhouses and meatpackers in the 1906 novel *The Jungle* caused a public outcry. It touched a nerve with Roosevelt, whose brigade had been supplied rancid canned meat during the Spanish-American War of 1898. By the end of 1906, Roosevelt had pushed through the Meat Inspection Act and the Pure Food and Drug Act, enforcing federal supervision of the food industry by the Bureau of Chemistry, which became the Food and Drug Administration in 1930.

WOODROW WILSON
December 28, 1856–February 3, 1924

Woodrow Wilson was born in Virginia to Scottish and Irish parents who supported both slavery and the Confederate States. Wilson did not learn to read until he was ten—possibly due to dyslexia—but he was an ambitious student. He studied at Princeton and then Johns Hopkins, and is to date the only American president with a Ph.D.

After eight years as president of Princeton University, Wilson entered politics as governor of New Jersey. His rise was meteoric: only two years later, in 1912, he was elected America's twenty-eighth president. He was a Progressive Democrat, and acted on his ideals during two terms in office. Votes for women, the Internal Revenue Service (IRS), and presidential press conferences are just part of his remarkable legacy. He also ushered the Federal Reserve System through Congress in 1913. His second term was overshadowed by America's reluctant involvement in World War One, but his ambitious plans for securing world peace earned him the Nobel Peace Prize in 1919.

Wilson's critics highlighted his high-handedness, however, citing his many interventions in Latin America, his sponsorship of two controversial wartime acts outlawing criticism of the government, and his support of racial segregation in various government offices, some of which had been integrated for fifty years.

Wilson suffered a stroke in 1919 and remained an invalid— although able to carry out his duties—until he left office in 1920. He retired in Washington, D.C., and died in 1924. Princeton honored him by establishing the Woodrow Wilson School of Public and International Affairs in 1930.

THE SIXTEENTH AMENDMENT: INCOME TAX
1913

The passing of the Sixteenth Amendment, which sanctioned income tax, was just one of a series of Progressive reforms introduced during Woodrow Wilson's administration and aimed at modernizing the way in which the federal government gathered revenue.

Income tax had briefly been introduced during the Civil War, and again in 1895, when it was labeled unconstitutional and thrown out by the Supreme Court. By the early twentieth century, Progressives felt that taxation on goods, imposed in the form of trade tariffs, unfairly disadvantaged those with low income, and they pushed for taxes to be levied according to income, so that the wealthier paid more than those earning less. Income tax was popular in the primarily agricultural states, whose citizens felt trade tariffs affected them disproportionately in comparison to the citizens of more industrial states.

Wilson's first response was to pass the Underwood Tariff, cutting the tariff on imported goods by 25 percent and eliminating it altogether in some cases, making imported goods more affordable. The Sixteenth Amendment soon followed, granting the federal government the right to levy taxes against income. This offset the loss of revenue from the Underwood Tariff. Wilson went on to establish the Federal Reserve System in 1913, and the Federal Trade Commission in 1914, which created central regulations for banking and commerce in order to try to stamp out corruption and monopolization.

THE PANAMA CANAL
1880–1914

The idea of a waterway connecting the Atlantic and Pacific oceans had been proposed as far back as the sixteenth century, when King Charles V of Spain commissioned plans for the construction of a canal that would reduce the voyage time of ships traveling to Peru.

In 1855, American contractors built the Panama Railroad across the Isthmus of Panama in order to address the dramatic increase of traffic into California during the Gold Rush. By bypassing the lengthy and precarious route around Cape Horn, the "transcontinental" railroad revolutionized coast-to-coast transportation, and was deemed such a success that interest in the feasibility of a canal was reawakened.

In 1869, President Ulysses S. Grant had several surveys carried out in Central America; in 1880, the French architect of the Suez Canal was charged with digging the Panama Canal alongside the route of the existing railway. Due to poor engineering plans and inhospitable conditions, thousands of workers died from malaria, equipment fell into decay, and the project failed miserably.

The Panama Canal project eventually became a reality under Theodore Roosevelt. Having supported Panama in its bid for independence from Colombia, the United States gained control over a ten-mile-wide zone, and work began in 1904. The canal cost $350 million to construct and was the largest and most difficult engineering project of its time. It was completed two years ahead of schedule, however, and first used in August 1914, reducing the journey time between the two oceans by more than half.

WORLD WAR ONE AND THE ROARING TWENTIES

AMERICA THE PEACE BROKER
1914

When a Serbian nationalist called Gavrilo Princip assassinated the Austro-Hungarian Archduke Franz Ferdinand in Sarajevo in June 1914, it ignited a catastrophic clash of the world's most powerful empires. Serbia enlisted Russian support in order to resist Austrian reprisal; Austria-Hungary sought and won German backing; Germany declared war on Russia and its Western European ally, France. The United Kingdom, reluctant at first to get involved, was forced to retaliate when the German army advanced through Belgium into France, to whom the United Kingdom was bound by a nineteenth-century protection treaty. In need of an Italian allegiance in order to attack Austria's southern borders, the United Kingdom persuaded Italy to join the war in 1915.

President Wilson recognized that participation in the war might ignite a powder keg in the United States. The majority of Americans were reluctant to be pulled into the war. Among those who were advocating American involvement, there was much disagreement over which side to support. A large proportion of American citizens were of either German or British descent. Other immigrant populations complicated the matter further still: Russian Jews would not condone American support of the nation by which they had been persecuted, while Irish immigrants, outraged by British suppression of the nationalist movement in Ireland, were opposed to Anglo-American allegiance.

Despite calls from Roosevelt and others to build up the US Army in preparation for war, Wilson chose the option most likely to safeguard the unity of his government—neutrality—and launched a diplomatic mission in hopes of mediating an end to the war.

THE *LUSITANIA* AND AMERICA'S DECLARATION OF WAR
1915–17

While President Wilson issued proclamations of American neutrality, American merchant ships continued to trade with the United Kingdom and Germany. In 1915, in response to a German U-boat campaign against British merchant ships in the Atlantic, the United Kingdom began transporting munitions by passenger ship, effectively making passenger ships fair game for German torpedoes. In early May, the German embassy in Washington issued warnings in the media to any American considering crossing the Atlantic aboard a British ship.

Days later, on May 7, 1915, the passenger liner RMS *Lusitania* was torpedoed by a German U-boat in the Atlantic. The ship sank in minutes, taking with it 128 American citizens among hundreds of others. Germany insisted the *Lusitania* had been loaded with armaments, a fact the British denied but which was later proven to be true. The attack was a decisive moment, and public pressure for war with Germany spread across the United States.

Wilson continued to work for a diplomatic resolution, a stance that won him reelection in 1916, but it soon became evident this was an unsustainable position. In February 1917, Germany began an unrestricted campaign against all shipping in the Atlantic. In April, the British intercepted the "Zimmermann Telegram," an order for the German ambassador in Mexico to seek a Mexican alliance with Germany. This move would have posed a direct European threat to the United States. Cornered into unplanned hostilities, Wilson asked Congress to declare war on Germany on April 2, 1917, asserting, "The world must be made safe for democracy."

MAKING THE WORLD SAFE
1917–18

Within weeks of entering the war, the Wilson administration passed the Selective Service Act, permitting the government to draft men between the ages of twenty-one and thirty for active military service. Conscription met with some objection, but the Espionage and Sedition Acts, passed as urgent war measures in 1917, made it illegal to speak out against the war effort and quickly silenced the most vocal.

In Europe, a Communist revolution headed by Vladimir Lenin led to Russia's withdrawal from the war in 1917. When American forces arrived in Europe in the spring of 1918, German troops had concentrated on the Western Front and were pushing the Allies back. The combined weight of American and Allied forces turned the tide; by September, exhausted German troops went into full retreat and Germany was forced to surrender, its civilians starved by an Allied blockade. The Kaiser abdicated in favor of a democratic Republic. The armistice came into effect at 11 a.m. on November 11, 1918— the eleventh hour of the eleventh day of the eleventh month—and peace was formally declared in the Treaty of Versailles of June 1919.

The cost of war was beyond anything anyone had imagined. The war had wiped out more than 10 million soldiers—an entire generation of young men. A further 20 million died from epidemics, particularly the "Spanish influenza," that ripped through trenches and war-torn communities. With the territorial ambitions of Germany, Austria-Hungary, and Turkey quashed, all that remained was to divide up the spoils and to negotiate a lasting peace.

THE IMPACT OF WAR AT HOME
1917–19

Although American involvement in World War One was without doubt a major factor in the defeat of Germany and the end of hostilities, Wilson's motives had not gone uncriticized. Detractors accused Washington and Wall Street of warmongering for financial gain, but Wilson spoke only of promoting democracy, an ideal to which the United States was committed. The fact remained, however, that wartime trade and industry helped the United States prosper, promoting the economy to unprecedented levels.

Wilson's war machine was slick: Wide-reaching federal regulations and a centrally engineered patriotism were fanned by a federal propaganda campaign and enforced by laws such as the Espionage and Sedition Acts, which made it a crime to convey or falsify information that might harm US Army operations, the war effort, or the government. Federal agencies supervised industry, transport, and agriculture in the name of efficiency, regulating anything that affected the war effort, from railroads to the manufacture of shoes. Suppliers' high profits were guaranteed, particularly those supplying munitions.

Rising wages, increased income and corporate taxes, and investment in popular Liberty Bonds funded the war and kept the economy buoyant, while a booming manufacturing industry served the growing demands of the American military. The net effect was economic prosperity and contentment that was unique among the warring nations. The United States emerged from the war in a stronger international position than ever before.

WILSON'S FOURTEEN POINTS
1918–19

In January 1918, confident of the Allied success to come, Wilson announced his fourteen-point plan for peace:

All diplomatic agreements should be made public.

International waters should remain navigable for all nations.

All economic barriers to international trade should be removed.

Armaments in all relevant countries should be scaled down.

Colonial disputes should be settled peacefully, and the right to self-determination granted to local populations.

All international troops should be evacuated from Russia.

Belgian independence should be restored.

Alsace-Lorraine should be restored to France.

The Italian borders should be restored.

The peoples of Austria-Hungary should become independent.

The independence of Romania, Serbia, and Montenegro should be established.

The Ottoman Empire should be divided according to nationality.

An independent Polish state should be established.

An international peacekeeping organization should be established.

When Wilson opened the Paris Peace Conference in January 1919, the British and French were in no mood for conciliation. Rejecting most of his fourteen points, they only agreed—eventually—to assert the independence of Belgium and Poland, to return Alsace-Lorraine to France, and to establish what became known as the League of Nations, and then the Treaty of Versailles was signed.

Back home, however, a Republican Congress did not favor the League and the Senate refused to ratify the Treaty. Deprived of vital American support, the League's chances of success were slim.

THE LEAGUE OF NATIONS AND A RETURN TO ISOLATIONISM
1919

The League of Nations, for which Wilson had such high hopes, was established in 1919, but without American support, it was at a huge disadvantage. More than that, the punitive nature of the terms of the Treaty of Versailles—which had ceded some of the richest industrial areas of Germany to France, for example—set the scene for lasting dissatisfaction in parts of Europe, the Middle East, and the Far East. In effect, even though it ended World War One, Versailles all but guaranteed future conflict.

The idealism inherent in Wilson's vision most concerned the American government. His dream of granting to all peoples the right to self-determination, or self-government, didn't sit easily with certain members of his administration. Secretary of State Robert Lansing, for example, warned of the "impossible demands" from every corner of the globe he believed would result from Wilson's ideology. Certainly numerous nations subjected to colonial rule, from Ireland to Vietnam, sent their envoys to Paris in 1919 to urge the assembled heads of state to establish their independence. All of them left disappointed.

Wilson's vision for lasting peace, in which he saw "the hand of God" at work, ultimately failed: Within two decades, the legacy of Versailles spawned World War Two. Moreover, the United States, wary of renewed entanglements in costly European wars, focused instead on rebuilding its own postwar infrastructure, and ultimately isolated itself not only from the League of Nations, but also from the international stage.

THE ROARING TWENTIES:
"THE AGE OF WONDERFUL NONSENSE"
1920–29

The end of World War One marked the beginning of a period of American prosperity and optimism. Industry continued to expand with the help of the country's huge reserve of raw materials, while higher import duties on foreign goods increased revenue.

The Ford Motor Company pioneered the moving assembly line in 1913, and mass production reduced the price of its Model T from $1,000 to $360. Other companies followed suit, and cheaper goods soon flooded the market. With the introduction of installment plans, ordinary Americans were able to afford telephones, radios, cars, and a host of labor-saving household appliances designed to liberate women from household drudgery. Consumerism had arrived, and the United States became the world's richest nation.

The Twenties were an era of hedonism and entertainment, featuring jazz music, theaters, "talkies"—non-silent movies—and a host of rising celebrities such as Charlie Chaplin, Al Jolson, and F. Scott Fitzgerald. Flapper girls challenged the traditional view of womanhood with their shorn hair, short hems, and casual use of cigarettes and makeup.

Perhaps surprisingly, all of this took place against the backdrop of Prohibition, a nationwide ban on the sale and consumption of alcohol. Bootlegging—the unlawful manufacture and traffic of alcohol—was controlled by organized crime syndicates, notably the Mafia, and gangster-run bars called "speakeasies" flourished.

PROHIBITION AND THE RISE OF THE MOB
1919–33

Since as far back as the seventeenth century, temperance movements—which were generally led by austere religious groups—had been growing in strength. By 1855, thirteen out of thirty-three states had been convinced to go "dry."

After the Civil War, groups such as the Woman's Christian Temperance Union and the Anti-Saloon League became increasingly influential. With women's rights activists and Progressive politicians joining the cause, Congress eventually—against the wishes of President Wilson—passed the Eighteenth Amendment in 1919. This stated: "The manufacture, sale, or transportation of intoxicating liquors within, the importation thereof into, or the exportation thereof from the United States and all territory subject to the jurisdiction thereof for beverage purposes is hereby prohibited."

People began brewing their own liquor ("moonshine") at home, and smuggling alcohol across the Mexican and Canadian borders. It was not long before organized crime syndicates such as the Mafia saw that there were millions to be made from bootlegging and the control of speakeasies (illegal bars). Mob culture was born, notorious gangsters such as Chicago rivals Al Capone and Bugs Moran rose to prominence, and mob warfare, murder, and retribution made headline news.

In 1933, under President Franklin D. Roosevelt, the Twenty-First Amendment repealed the Eighteenth, and Prohibition was ended.

THE GREAT
DEPRESSION
AND WORLD
WAR TWO

THE WALL STREET CRASH
October 1929

The excesses of the Roaring Twenties gave the United States an inflated sense of wealth and financial liberty. It was only a matter of time before this illusion would be shattered.

The banks upheld public optimism, convincing the middle classes that, with a little spare cash, wealth was within their grasp. They encouraged investors to invest "on the margin," paying for just 10 percent of the shares they wanted and taking out a loan for the rest. Once shares had risen in value, the investor would sell them, pay off the bank loan, and still make a profit. It was an easy gamble, and a highly addictive cycle while share prices continued to rise. Each new profit became another 10 percent down payment on a bigger investment.

By October 1929, $8.5 billion was on loan from American banks. A few canny bankers realized that, if shares ever took a wholesale tumble, the investment bubble would burst; nervously, they began to sell. Other investors grew anxious: Had the big banks sniffed trouble? In a matter of days, panic swept through Wall Street; by "Black Tuesday," October 29, everyone was selling. Share prices crashed and $30 billion was lost overnight.

The impact of the crash was devastating. Share prices continued to fall, and the numerous banks that had gambled their deposits on the stock market were destroyed, depriving thousands of their life savings. The country was soon in the grip of the worst depression in its history.

THE GREAT DEPRESSION
1930s

During the depression that followed the 1929 Crash, more than 5,000 banks were shut down, and the hard-earned savings of countless people disappeared. Meanwhile, with no borrowing or credit available, factories and corporations were forced to close their doors. At its most severe points, around 25 percent of America's workforce was left jobless. No wages meant that mortgages and rents went unpaid, and the number of homeless people increased daily, as homes were repossessed by the banks.

President Hoover's response to the crisis was wholly ineffectual. Believing that a new prosperity was just around the corner, he failed to recognize the vast scale of the problem—even when cardboard shantytowns dubbed "Hoovervilles" appeared across the country. His support for the Smoot-Hawley Tariff Act of 1930, which raised tariffs on imported items in an attempt to boost sales of American produce, backfired when foreign countries raised tariffs on American exports. Relief programs offered little respite: Hoover refused to give direct federal aid, insisting that local governments help with local needs. But local governments had no money.

The depression deepened and people began dying from poverty, starvation, and disease, while the suicide rate rocketed. In Texas, Oklahoma, and surrounding states, the problem was compounded throughout the 1930s by the "Dust Bowl"—dust storms and barren farmland caused by severe drought and years of bad land management—and millions were forced to flee westward.

By 1932, Americans had had enough and elected Franklin D. Roosevelt as president. His promise of a "New Deal" to haul the nation from the depths of despair offered a glimmer of hope.

HERBERT C. HOOVER
August 10, 1874–October 20, 1964

Born in Iowa and orphaned by the age of nine, Herbert Hoover was raised by his parents' relatives. In 1891, he joined the first intake of students at Stanford University, where he excelled at sports and earned a degree in geology.

As a leading mining engineer, Hoover worked in Australia and then China, where he and his wife, Lou Henry Hoover, learned to speak Mandarin. His humanitarian tendencies first came to light during the 1900 Boxer Rebellion, when he risked his life to rescue a number of Chinese children.

During World War One, Hoover engaged in tireless European relief efforts, and was appointed head of the Food Administration—a wartime commission aimed at avoiding food shortage or wastage—by President Wilson. When he was accused of Bolshevism for sending aid to famine-stricken Russians, he responded: "Twenty million people are starving. Whatever their politics, they shall be fed!"

Hoover joined the Republican Party and rose through the ranks, serving as secretary of commerce under Presidents Harding and Coolidge. In 1928, he ran for president, pronouncing that the United States "has come nearer to the abolition of poverty . . . than humanity has ever reached before." Less than a year after his election, the stock market crashed, and the Great Depression soon followed. As homelessness and unemployment increased, Hoover's lack of direct action and ineffectual relief programs turned him from humanitarian into scapegoat, and he suffered a humiliating defeat in his bid for reelection in 1932.

Hoover spent his later years enjoying the American countryside, and wrote several books. He died in New York, aged ninety.

FRANKLIN D. ROOSEVELT
January 30, 1882–April 12, 1945

Franklin Delano Roosevelt—later known as "FDR"—was born in New York. He had a privileged upbringing, attending Groton School and later Harvard University. When his fifth cousin Theodore Roosevelt became president in 1901, it ignited the political ambition in young Franklin.

In 1905, Roosevelt married Theodore's niece Eleanor, and they went on to have six children. He passed the New York State Bar exam and became a Wall Street lawyer, but his charisma and social adeptness soon led him into politics: He became a senator of New York in 1911, assistant secretary of the Navy in 1913, and Democratic vice presidential nominee in 1920, although he was unsuccessful in this bid.

In the summer of 1921, Roosevelt faced the biggest challenge of his life when he was incapacitated by what was believed to be polio. Paralyzed from the waist down, he nevertheless refused to accept a lifetime in a wheelchair; with heroic determination, he learned to walk using crutches, and even to drive a specially adapted car.

Despite ongoing ill health, Roosevelt became governor of New York in 1930, and was elected to the first of a record-breaking four presidential terms in 1932. With the United States in the grip of the Great Depression, he promised action and solutions, declaring in his inaugural address: "The only thing we have to fear is fear itself."

FDR is best remembered for his "New Deal," for ending Prohibition, and for directing America through World War Two. On April 12, 1945, one month before the European ceasefire he had passionately worked toward, Roosevelt died of a cerebral hemorrhage while still in office.

THE NEW DEAL
1932–36

In 1932, a Depression-ravaged America looked to President Roosevelt to kick-start the economy with his campaign promise of a "New Deal;" in his first hundred days in office, Roosevelt passed an incredible range of radical legislation through Congress. A "Second New Deal" in 1935 introduced further reforms.

The Federal Deposit Insurance Corporation (FDIC) was created to protect and insure savings and restore confidence in the beleaguered banking system; the Home Owners' Loan Corporation made funding available to those facing the loss of their homes; and the Civilian Conservation Corps created projects in the national forests and parks that put hundreds of thousands of Americans back into gainful employment.

One of the most controversial schemes, the National Industrial Recovery Act, was devised to boost industrial production by allowing manufacturers to set their own prices, while at the same time regulating workers' minimum wages and maximum hours. The act angered private industries, was rife for abuse, and did little to increase production or keep prices low.

The agricultural industry, however, was helped by a program of federal subsidies and innovative reforms. The Tennessee Valley Authority, for example, built dams, roads, and hydroelectric plants in the most needy of America's states, as well as training farmers in better land management. The modernization of Tennessee's infrastructure also brought industries and jobs to the state.

It would take another world war to fully restore America's economy, but the New Deal did at least succeed in boosting morale and the nation's confidence in its government.

AMERICAN ISOLATION AND THE THREAT OF WAR
1930s

In the early 1930s, while Roosevelt was preventing a Depression-hit United States from descending into chaos, Europe was also suffering the effects of the global downturn, and hostility between desperate nations was starting to brew. While Italy had become a single-party Fascist state under Benito Mussolini, Germany—virtually paralyzed by the Treaty of Versailles—turned to Nazi Party leader Adolf Hitler for salvation. Blaming Marxists, foreign powers, and Jews for Germany's economic distress, Hitler was soon arming Germany to the hilt in preparation for a renewed military entrance onto the world stage.

At home, however, a noninterventionist policy prevailed in Congress. Hoping to prevent the United States from becoming embroiled in yet another European war, leading senators pushed through a series of Neutrality Acts during the 1930s. President Roosevelt argued that a blanket policy of nonintervention might in fact provide passive assistance to enemies of America's allies, but he was outnumbered.

The four Neutrality Acts of 1935–39 collectively placed an embargo on all trade with warring nations, and forbade American citizens from traveling to war zones. When Roosevelt saw that allies of the United States were in desperate need of help against countries pursuing aggressive expansionist agendas—China against Japan in 1937, the United Kingdom against Germany in 1939—he employed loopholes that allowed limited trade on a selective basis, but was unable to force a change in foreign policy. American neutrality effectively remained in place until the nation came under direct attack in 1941.

THE OUTBREAK OF WORLD WAR TWO
September 3, 1939

The United States officially remained isolationist through the Spanish Civil War of 1936–39, despite many Americans joining the losing fight for the Spanish loyalist cause. As the war raged on, the United Kingdom and France—fearing the fighting would erupt into all-out war—also stayed on the sidelines. Others were less hesitant: Mussolini and Hitler eagerly assisted Spain's General Franco and his Fascist rebels against Spain's republican government, which in turn was aided by the Soviet Union.

Across the world in Asia, Japan had already defied a 1922 pledge to uphold China's territorial rights by invading Manchuria in 1931, and withdrew from the League of Nations two years later. In 1936, Japan signed an anti-Communist pact with Germany, and attacked China once again in July 1937.

Back in Europe, Hitler—who had already breached the Treaty of Versailles by marching troops back into the Rhineland—invaded Austria in 1938 and reincorporated it into Germany. He then demanded the return of Sudetenland, which had merged with Czechoslovakia after World War One. The United Kingdom and France agreed to his demands but woefully misjudged the situation; buoyed by their acquiescence, Hitler seized the rest of Czechoslovakia and went on to invade Poland on September 1, 1939. The United Kingdom and France declared war on Germany two days later.

President Roosevelt, frustrated by the Neutrality Acts, went against isolationist policy by introducing the Lend-Lease Act of 1941. This allowed the United States to lend war equipment to any nation "whose defense the President deems vital to the defense of the United States."

PEARL HARBOR
December 7, 1941

Relations between the United States and Japan, already uneasy due to Japan's aggressive foreign policy through the 1920s, became tenser still following Japan's attacks on China. In 1937, Japan declared all-out war on China—whose disorganized military was no match for Japan's imperial might—and formed the Tripartite Pact with Italy and Germany three years later. Japan then invaded French Indochina in an effort to gain access to valuable natural resources in Southeast Asia.

President Roosevelt, hoping to deter Japanese hostilities, issued an embargo on exports of oil and raw materials to Japan. This action, combined with the transfer of the US Pacific Fleet from San Diego to Pearl Harbor, Hawaii—almost midway between the United States and Japan—was viewed as a threat to Japanese ambitions.

Intending to strike a blow at the heart of American morale and prevent American interference in a planned southward expansion, 350 Japanese aircraft and a number of submarines destroyed and damaged a significant proportion of the Pacific Fleet on the morning of Sunday December 7, 1941. Four battleships, three cruisers, three destroyers, and one minelayer were sunk, and more than 200 grounded American aircraft were wiped out. Around 2,400 American personnel were killed and over 1,200 wounded.

The following day, Congress made a formal declaration of war against Japan, and Roosevelt stated that, "No matter how long it may take us to overcome this premeditated invasion, the American people, in their righteous might, will win through to absolute victory." Three days later, Japan's allies Germany and Italy declared war on the United States.

THE DARKEST WEEKS
December 1941–January 1942

A merica's major allies in the war against the "Axis powers" of
Japan, Germany, and Italy were the United Kingdom, the
Soviet Union, Australia, and China. With the Japanese rampaging
through the Pacific while Hitler and Mussolini advanced through
Europe, there were two simultaneous fronts to fight.

In the immediate aftermath of Pearl Harbor, Japan launched a
series of air raids on the American territory of Guam and on the US
Marine base at Wake Island. The Japanese invasion fleet then struck
Wake Island twice, the first occasion being the only amphibious
attack of the war to be driven back by shore-based weapons. This
small but short-lived victory provided a much-needed boost to
American morale during Japan's continued strikes on American-held
territories in the Pacific. The British colony of Hong Kong was in
Japanese hands by Christmas Day 1941, and was soon joined by the
Dutch East Indies, Burma, Singapore, and British Malaya.

As Japan prepared to take control of the Philippines, the largest
mobilization of American troops to date was taking place. Between
January 1942 and early 1944, 120,000 American troops had passed
through Northern Ireland on their way to mainland Europe. Back at
home, the Great Depression came to a sudden end as the nation's
factories filled with new workers and set about providing everything
from food to armaments.

With Japan viewed as a particular threat, Japanese-Americans
were classified as enemy aliens, rounded up by the FBI, and moved
to internment camps, where they were stripped of their rights as
American citizens. No such action was taken against German-
Americans or Italian-Americans.

BATAAN AND THE DEATH MARCH
1942

Japan's plan to control the Southwest Pacific and gain control of the Dutch East Indies with all its resources called for a wave of simultaneous strikes on Malaya, Thailand, Hawaii, Hong Kong, Singapore, Guam, Wake, and most crucially, the Philippine Islands.

With a significant proportion of the US Pacific Fleet out of action due to the bombing at Pearl Harbor, it was left to American and Filipino forces—the USAFFE—to defend the islands from the ground. Pitted against the superior Japanese Fourteenth Army and with no lines of supply or escape, there was little that they could do to prevent the Japanese onslaught. By the end of December 1941, Luzon, the largest and most strategically important island of the Philippines, was almost entirely in the hands of the Japanese. The USAFFE, under the command of General Douglas MacArthur, was forced to put into action a prewar defense plan to retreat in order to continue defending Corregidor and the Bataan Peninsula while waiting for reinforcements.

Reinforcements never arrived; on April 9, 1942, after four months of valiant fighting, Commanding General Edward King had to surrender over 70,000 besieged and overwhelmed Philippine and American troops to the Japanese.

Now prisoners of war, the battle-weary, undernourished, and weak American Army was forced to march out of Bataan to prison camps over seventy miles away. The Death March of Bataan resulted in the deaths of between 6,000 and 11,000 prisoners, due to the brutal and inhumane treatment they received at the hands of their Japanese captors.

THE BATTLE OF MIDWAY
June 1942

The Battle of Midway is regarded by many as having been the turning point of the war in the Pacific, signaling the beginning of the end for Japan's bid for supremacy in East Asia.

On March 13, 1942, the Office of Naval Intelligence, having intercepted Japanese radio communications, succeeded in breaking the Japanese Navy's General Purpose Code, giving Allied commanders in the Pacific crucial forewarning of Japanese plans. With this knowledge, American forces were able to damage at least twenty-five Japanese vessels in the Battle of the Coral Sea on May 7–8, 1942, and to halt a Japanese invasion attempt.

The Japanese had hoped to draw the US Fleet's remaining carriers into a decisive conflict at Midway, securing the American outpost as a strategic defense position and bringing the US Fleet to its knees. But when American cryptanalysts identified Midway Island as Japan's next target, with a predicted attack date of June 4, 1942, the Fleet's commander in chief, Admiral Chester W. Nimitz, had time to formulate his counteroffensive.

From June 4–7, 1942, the pre-warned US Fleet engaged in fierce battle with the Japanese Navy, sinking four of its six carriers, three destroyers, and two cruisers, and destroying three hundred planes. The Japanese fleet sustained extensive damage, severely curbing Japan's ambitions for Pacific expansion.

THE WAR AT HOME
1940–45

While American forces were fighting in Europe and Asia, a major war effort was under way at home. Following the Great Depression of the 1930s, America's fortunes were transformed by increased international demand in the early 1940s, and the country's industrial output rocketed just as its young men were sent to war.

Women played a vital role, taking on jobs traditionally filled by men. This was especially evident in the booming manufacturing industries, with women brought in to produce munitions and other military supplies. The image of "Rosie the Riveter"—the iconic character used in propaganda of the period—encouraged millions of women to take on factory, agricultural, and clerical jobs vacated by men, and ultimately helped modernize perceptions of a woman's role in the family.

Even before Pearl Harbor, a group of high-profile women pilots led by Nancy Harkness Love had proposed that they fly non-combat missions for the US Air Force, such as delivering airplanes and supplies, so that their male counterparts would be available for combat. The proposal was accepted and the association of female pilots eventually formalized as the Women Airforce Service Pilots (WASP), with over 300 women employed during the war.

On a smaller but equally vital scale, homeowners across the nation followed First Lady Eleanor Roosevelt's example by planting "Victory Gardens," fruit and vegetable plots designed to ease the pressure on America's farmers and food supply chain, and to "sow the seeds of victory." These schemes allowed American industries to run more efficiently, and provided a welcome boost in morale.

THE ALLIED INVASIONS OF
NORTH AFRICA AND ITALY
1942–44

One of the largest invasions in history—code-named Operation Torch—was carried out by American and British forces in November 1942. Over 100,000 men and 600 ships landed on the coast of North Africa. Although the Axis forces far outnumbered the Allies and the fighting was ferocious, Tunis was in Allied hands by May 7, 1943. With North Africa secured, the way was clear for an invasion of Italy; Roosevelt and British prime minister Winston Churchill had made the decision to attack Europe through its "soft underbelly" at a secret conference in Casablanca earlier that year.

On July 10, 1943, American and British troops landed on the island of Sicily and put Operation Husky into action. Facing stiff resistance from German troops, the Allies nevertheless achieved their goal, securing Sicily by the middle of August.

The planned invasion of the Italian mainland went ahead despite the fact that Mussolini had been overthrown the day before Sicily was taken. German resistance was heavy, and it was not until the beginning of October that southern Italy came under Allied control. The Germans, determined not to allow Rome to be taken, formed their heavily defended "Winter Line," which stretched the width of central Italy and proved almost impregnable. But after more than six months of persistent assaults, the Allies finally broke through the line, and captured Rome on June 5, 1944.

D-DAY
June 6, 1944

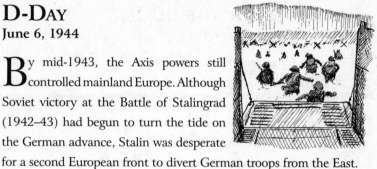

By mid-1943, the Axis powers still controlled mainland Europe. Although Soviet victory at the Battle of Stalingrad (1942–43) had begun to turn the tide on the German advance, Stalin was desperate for a second European front to divert German troops from the East.

With the invasion of Italy well under way, Roosevelt, Stalin, and Churchill met to discuss military strategy in November 1943 in Tehran, Iran, a location chosen for its proximity to the Soviet Union, to ensure that the anxious Stalin would attend. They agreed to mount a major invasion of France—code-named Operation Overlord—in the hope of regaining access to Europe. General Dwight D. Eisenhower, one of the war's most powerful military figures, was given command of the top-secret offensive, whose date was referred to as "D-Day."

On June 6, 1944, American, British and Canadian forces landed simultaneously on five beaches in Normandy, France. It was the largest and most powerful amphibious force ever assembled, numbering 150,000 troops and some 7,000 vessels. The Germans were taken by surprise, as radar deception and decoy radio transmissions had led them to believe the invasion would take place farther north, in Calais. Nonetheless, Allied forces were faced with a ruthless opposition of around fifty divisions of the German Army, and approximately 2,500 Allied troops were killed on D-Day alone.

But the invasion and the ensuing Battle of Normandy were a great success. By the end of August 1944, Paris was reclaimed by the Allies, France was liberated, and Hitler's downfall was in sight.

THE BATTLE OF THE BULGE
December 1944–January 1945

German forces had been in retreat following the success of the Normandy landings and the liberation of Paris and Brussels. The Allies continued to advance toward Germany, and when the US First Army captured the German city of Eupen on October 21, 1944, it seemed that Hitler had all but lost the war.

Unable to face defeat, Hitler launched an ill-advised offensive against the Allies, hoping to break through the front line at the Ardennes Mountains and ultimately capture the Belgian port of Antwerp, through which the Allies were receiving supplies. But with his army virtually depleted of fuel and supplies, it was a plan born of desperation.

On the morning of December 16, 1944, the German attack began. The unsuspecting Allies were subjected to an initial two-hour bombardment, and, with heavy fog and cloud keeping Allied planes grounded, the Germans managed to push westward through the Ardennes Mountains, creating a "bulge" in the front line and inflicting heavy losses on the Allied forces.

By December 22, the skies had cleared and the Allies brought their superior air force into play, swiftly stalling the German advance. The ensuing "Battle of the Bulge" was fought in extreme weather conditions, with cold and rain leading to many cases of exposure and trench foot, a painful condition caused by lengthy immersion in water. By mid-January 1945, the Germans had run out of fuel; with the bulge driven back eastward by the US First and Third Armies, the largest and bloodiest battle fought by American troops in World War Two was the last throw of the dice by the Nazi war machine.

VE DAY
May 8, 1945

By early 1945, Hitler's fight for Europe was effectively over. Having sustained critical losses on the Western front, the Germans were also struggling against the Soviet offensive that was sweeping across the East, reclaiming territories overtaken by Hitler in 1939.

American troops, under the command of General Eisenhower, were advancing along the western bank of the Rhine. Some of the bloodiest fighting of the war took place as the Allies confronted German soldiers still guarding the "Siegfried Line," a line of heavily armed tanks and bunkers along the German border.

On March 7, 1945, the US First Army captured the Ludendorff Bridge across the Rhine at Remagen, after a failed German attempt to blow it up. American troops established a bridgehead and executed a full-scale crossing. On March 22, the US Third Army crossed the Rhine south of Mainz at Oppenheim, and the Allies spread out into western Germany.

By the end of April, the major cities of Nuremburg and Leipzig had fallen, and the US First Army and the Soviets had joined forces at the River Elbe. On April 30, in Soviet-overrun Berlin, Hitler committed suicide in his bunker. The following week, on May 8, 1945, Germany officially surrendered to the Western Allies and the Soviet Union, and the date was declared "Victory in Europe Day," or VE Day.

The United States, in mourning for the recently deceased President Roosevelt, now looked for an end to the war still raging in the Pacific.

GUADALCANAL AND SOUTH PACIFIC ISLAND HOPPING
1942–45

Following Japanese defeat at the Battle of Midway in 1942, control of air space over the Solomon Islands became crucial to America's plans to retake the Philippines. The small South Pacific island of Guadalcanal, on which the Japanese had already begun constructing an airfield, was the first target in a successful campaign of "island-hopping" strikes designed to capture key Japanese-held territory prior to an invasion of mainland Japan.

On August 7, 1942, Allied ground, sea, and air forces, led by General Douglas MacArthur in the Southwest Pacific and Admiral Chester W. Nimitz of the Pacific Fleet, attacked Guadalcanal and began a grueling six-month battle that ultimately ended in defeat for Imperial Japan.

With Guadalcanal under American control, MacArthur directed his drive along the New Guinea coast, and Nimitz pushed across the central Pacific. The island of Tarawa fell to the United States in November 1943, followed by Saipan in July 1944. Victory proved costly, with the deaths of nearly 3,000 Americans and almost an entire garrison of Japanese troops, while hundreds of Japanese civilians chose suicide over surrender. Guam was secured in August 1944, and the heavily fortified island of Iwo Jima was eventually won in March 1945, after some of the fiercest fighting of the campaign.

After taking Okinawa Island in June 1945, the Allies were in a position to invade mainland Japan, and an invasion strategy was formulated.

THE BATTLE OF LEYTE GULF
October 1944

While Admiral Nimitz's South Pacific "island-hopping" campaign was racking up victories, General MacArthur, more than 1,000 miles to the south, had recaptured the Solomon Islands and New Guinea, securing the Japanese air and naval base at Rabaul in the Battle of the Bismarck Sea.

While Nimitz believed that the next move against the Japanese Empire should be the capture of the island of Formosa, General MacArthur advocated the liberation of the Philippines. With the intervention of President Roosevelt, the Allied forces set their sights on an invasion of Leyte, one of the largest islands of the Philippines.

The attack on Leyte was led by the US Third Fleet under the command of Admiral William Halsey. Beginning on October 23, 1944, the Battle of Leyte Gulf was the largest naval battle in history, engaging some 300 vessels in three days of heavy fighting.

Despite deploying the full force of its remaining naval strength against the Allies, the already depleted Japanese Imperial Navy was all but decimated by the loss of 10,000 men. For the first time in the war, Japanese pilots resorted to kamikaze attacks in an attempt to destroy American battleships and aircraft carriers. It was to no avail, and the Japanese were defeated at sea. With the enemy's power in steady decline, landed Allied forces were able to push across the Philippines, liberating the capital Manila on March 3, 1945.

HIROSHIMA AND NAGASAKI
August 1945

In retaliation for Pearl Harbor, the United States had engaged in a major bombing campaign over Tokyo in April 1942. A second major campaign began in early 1945, aimed at grinding down Japanese morale prior to a planned invasion of the mainland, which, it was hoped, would finally end the war.

As preparations for the invasion continued, physicist J. Robert Oppenheimer and his New Mexico–based scientific research team, the Manhattan Project, completed three years of extensive research into nuclear warheads. They tested the world's first atomic bomb at Los Alamos on July 16.

Peace negotiations stalled that summer, with Japan dismissing President Truman's ultimatum to "surrender or suffer prompt and utter destruction." Determined to force Japan's military ambitions into total collapse, as well as to show the world—particularly the Soviets—the awesome new power of the United States, Truman authorized the use of atomic bombs over Japan.

On August 6, a B-29 bomber dropped a ten-foot uranium-235 bomb, "Little Boy," over Hiroshima, demolishing two-thirds of the city. Faced with continued Japanese resistance, a second bomber was dispatched three days later, and dropped a plutonium-239 bomb code-named "Fat Man" over Nagasaki. The bombs killed as many as 220,000 civilians instantly, while many others died later from the effects of radiation.

On August 15, Emperor Hirohito surrendered to the Allies; he signed the Instrument of Surrender on September 2. One day short of its sixth anniversary, World War Two was over.

WAR CRIMES AND THE CREATION
OF THE STATE OF ISRAEL
1939–48

Although the war was officially over, the legacy of its bloodiest and most bloodthirsty episodes presented the Allies with an urgent and difficult problem: how to ensure that such atrocities were never committed again. The public denouncement and punishment of German and Japanese leaders was an obvious place to start, and a number of high-profile figures were tried for war crimes and crimes against humanity, notably at the Nuremberg Trials of 1945 to 1949, and the Tokyo Tribunal of 1946.

The most notorious war crime of World War Two was the Holocaust, authorized by Hitler and responsible for the deaths of 6 million European Jews, as well as millions of other prisoners. Interred in dozens of Eastern European concentration camps, prisoners were forced into hard labor, subjected to cold and harsh conditions, and ultimately killed by disease, starvation, or mass extermination. A number of detainees were experimented upon by German scientists looking for advances in medicine and biological and chemical warfare, a barbarous practice also undertaken over an eight-year period by Unit 731 of the Imperial Japanese Army, mainly on Chinese prisoners.

The mass displacement of Jews caused by the Holocaust—and the reluctance of many countries to provide a permanent safe haven for them—led to millions of Jews emigrating to Palestine, where, in May 1948, they declared independence as the state of Israel. The United States was the first country to recognize and support the new nation, an attitude that continues to inform American foreign policy.

POSTWAR
AMERICA

THE UNITED NATIONS
1942–45

The name "United Nations" was originally used by President Franklin Roosevelt in reference to the World War Two Allies, united in their fight against the Axis powers. On January 1, 1942, representatives of twenty-six countries signed the Declaration by United Nations, which pledged to continue this fight. At a conference of foreign ministers in October 1943, the remit of the United Nations was extended to include international peacekeeping, as a replacement for the ineffectual League of Nations.

The following year, representatives from the United States, the United Kingdom, the Soviet Union, and China met for the Dumbarton Oaks Conference in Washington, D.C. Their task was to thrash out the details of what would become the new world governing body of the United Nations. The main issues discussed were the structure and makeup of the Security Council and its use of the power of veto, and the Soviet Union's insistence upon separate membership for sixteen of its republics. At the beginning of February 1945, these issues were again discussed, and eventually resolved, at a meeting between the "Big Three"—Roosevelt, Churchill, and Stalin—at Yalta, in the Crimea.

Delegates from fifty nations that had been at war with Germany met in April through June of 1945, to draft and adopt the first United Nations Charter. The Charter was ratified in London on October 24, 1945, at the first session of the General Assembly of the United Nations; the world's most important peacekeeping body was born. The United Nations met at various locations until its new headquarters in New York City was completed in 1952.

HARRY S. TRUMAN
May 8, 1884–December 26, 1972

Born to a farmer and livestock dealer, Harry S. Truman was educated and brought up in Independence, Missouri. After serving in the National Guard during his twenties, he reenlisted at age thirty-three when the United States joined World War One, and fought in France.

On his return, Truman went into the haberdashery business. His Kansas City store was severely hit by the 1921 recession, however, and Truman left small business to join the Democratic Party and become a judge of Jackson County Court.

In 1934, Truman was elected to the Senate, a position he retained for ten years. During World War Two, he headed the Truman Committee, investigating waste of funding and resources in the US Army, and ultimately saved the nation around $15 billion. Having demonstrated his leadership and political integrity, he became Roosevelt's vice president in 1945, just eighty-two days before the president died in office.

On assuming the presidency, Truman had scant knowledge of ongoing wartime tactics, let alone the development of the atomic bomb, and told journalists, "I felt like the moon, the stars, and all the planets had fallen on me." Despite its chaotic beginnings, his presidency included some of the most significant events in political history: the nuclear bombing of Japan, the founding of the United Nations, the Marshall Plan, and the Korean War. Taking difficult matters in his stride, Truman popularized the phrase "The buck stops here."

He retired in 1952 to write his memoirs, and died in Missouri twenty years later, at age eighty-eight.

THE "SUPERPOWERS"
1945–90

Although hundreds of thousands of American troops lost their lives in World War Two, the nation emerged relatively unscathed. Advances in weaponry, communications, transportation, electronics, and medicine had accelerated during the war, the huge demand for military and industrial exports had resulted in a vast and prosperous manufacturing capability, and the economy was booming.

The Soviet Union, on the other hand, had suffered terribly, with huge swaths of the country destroyed and many prewar industries taken into enemy hands. Nonetheless, it remained in a better strategic position than any other European power, occupying all of Eastern and Central Europe, and boasting a large military that had been well and truly battle-tested.

By the end of the war, it was only these two powerful victors—the "superpowers"—who stood out on the international arena. Their ideologies differed wildly, however, which not only forced a schism between the former allies, but also led to an unprecedented struggle for international supremacy.

Following the United States' incredible display of nuclear might in August 1945, the race was on to develop bigger and deadlier weapons. Between 1946 and 1958, the United States carried out over 100 nuclear tests in the atolls of the Pacific, while the Soviet Union caused international alarm when it tested its first hydrogen bomb, a twenty-seven-ton weapon nicknamed Tsar Bomba, in October 1961. Although the bomb was too large to be practical for warfare, the superpowers had for the first time—and at the height of their political and military rivalry—developed weapons with the terrifying power to destroy the world.

THE IRON CURTAIN
1945–90

While the United States, the United Kingdom, and France wanted to avoid harsh treatment of Germany, the Soviet Union was out for total revenge. As a temporary compromise, the four countries divided Germany into four zones and controlled one each. The capital city, Berlin, situated in Soviet-controlled East Germany, was similarly divided into four, with the Western allies occupying West Berlin and the Soviet Union taking East Berlin.

Determined to rebuild occupied countries in the Soviet Union's image, Stalin began gathering Eastern European countries into a Communist, Soviet-dominated "Eastern bloc." He faced vehement opposition from the countries of Western Europe but was particularly troubled by the United States, whose international influence and military might he was determined to outdo.

In March 1946, former British prime minister Winston Churchill gave one of his most famous postwar speeches, stating that, "From Stettin in the Baltic to Trieste in the Adriatic an iron curtain has descended across the Continent." This speech popularized the phrase "iron curtain," which was used for the next fifty years to describe the military, social, and economic barriers created by the Soviet Union during what political analysts labeled the "Cold War."

The iron curtain exacerbated the already frosty relations between the superpowers, but the threat of Mutually Assured Destruction—MAD—that accompanied the nuclear age essentially restricted the Cold War to a conflict of resolve rather than of military confrontation. This state of hostility did, however, spur on "proxy wars" between the United States and its Soviet-supported Communist enemies, such as the Bay of Pigs Invasion, and the Korean and Vietnam Wars.

THE MARSHALL PLAN
1947

In March 1947, before a joint session of Congress, President Truman proposed providing American support to the Greek government in its fight against Communism. This foreign policy turnaround from isolationism to international intervention developed into the Truman Doctrine, which pledged military, economic, and political support for "free peoples who are resisting attempted subjugation by armed minorities or by outside pressure."

The following month, in a bid to further promote the growth of democracy and to resist the spread of Communism, Secretary of State George C. Marshall announced plans for a program of American aid to fund the rebuilding of war-ravaged Europe. "It is logical that the United States should do whatever it is able to do to assist in the return of normal economic health in the world, without which there can be no political stability and no assured peace. Our policy is directed not against any country or doctrine but against hunger, poverty, desperation, and chaos."

The Marshall Plan offered financial aid not only to former allies but also to former enemies. Rejected by the Soviet Union, which was wary of losing its immense power over Eastern Europe, the Marshall Plan nevertheless went on to spend some $12.5 billion during its three-year existence, helping to bring economic and political stability to Western Europe and greatly reducing the spread of Communist influence.

THE BERLIN AIRLIFT
June 24, 1948–May 11, 1949

Both the Soviet Union and the Western allies realized the political value of shaping postwar Berlin. While the Western allies were determined to merge their three zones into a democratic "West Berlin," they were hampered by the fact that Berlin was situated in the middle of Soviet-controlled East Germany, and by Stalin's determination to keep Germany weak.

When the Western allies introduced a new, stronger currency, the Deutsche Mark, Stalin refused to recognize either the currency or the independence of West Berlin, and became increasingly intolerant of the economic resurgence that was threatening to revitalize Germany. In an effort to bring West Berlin to its knees, and ultimately to take control of it before Western influence became fixed, Stalin blocked all rail and road access into the city, preventing the supply of food and fuel. The Berlin Blockade was the first crisis of the Cold War.

Determined neither to relinquish West Berlin nor to bend to Soviet pressure, President Truman ordered an emergency airlift along previously agreed air corridors. It was a massive undertaking, but over a ten-month period, an estimated 2,245,300 tons of food and fuel supplies were delivered to citizens and troops in West Berlin. For almost a year, the city depended on the Western allies for everything from candy to coal.

The operation proved to be a political victory for the West. On May 11, 1949, a humiliated Soviet Union lifted the futile blockade, and democratic West Berlin became a permanent satellite of West Germany.

THE McCARTHY WITCH HUNTS
1950–54

On February 9, 1950, controversial Republican senator Joseph McCarthy initiated an anti-Communist witch hunt following an incendiary speech at the Republican Women's Club of Wheeling, West Virginia. Claiming to have a list of up to 205 State Department employees who were members of the American Communist Party—a list later proven to be fictitious—McCarthy brought the threat of Communism closer to home than many had dared imagine. His allegations made him a household name overnight, and the term "McCarthyism," invoking a policy of finger pointing, was soon coined.

For four years, McCarthy led an obsessive campaign to uncover the identities of "suspected" Communist government employees, claiming that many were acting as Soviet spies. Where he had conviction, he often lacked proof; nevertheless, the prevailing climate meant that even an allegation of Communism could destroy a career. Hundreds of Hollywood figures with former or suspected Communist sympathies were blacklisted for their "un-American activities." Playwright Arthur Miller was notably blacklisted, while Charlie Chaplin had his right to United States residence revoked.

In 1953, McCarthy was made chairman of the Senate Committee on Government Operations, and whipped up anti-Communist hysteria by conducting very public investigations into esteemed institutions including the US Army. Smear tactics were used against the Democrats and over 30,000 "pro-Communist" books were removed from libraries.

McCarthy's total fabrication of most of his "evidence" eventually led to him being discredited by the press and the Senate, although he retained his position until his death, aged forty-eight, in May 1957.

THE KOREAN WAR:
THE SEEDS ARE SOWN
1950

After the defeat of Japan in August 1945, the Japanese-occupied Korean Peninsula was divided up between the United States and the Soviet Union, along the thirty-eighth parallel.

The division was intended as a temporary measure until an independent Korean government could be installed. But when Korea's reunification was discussed, it became clear that the ideologies of the occupying nations would clash. While the United States wanted an approved, democratic South Korean government to spread north, Stalin was intent on claiming North Korea as a Communist territory. He ordered the Red Army to fortify the thirty-eighth parallel and refused to enter into discussions with the United States on the formation of a Korean government.

The United Nations intervened and, despite Soviet objections, ruled that an election should be held and that the new government would have its independence protected by a United Nations security force. But resistance from North Korean Communists meant that the elections took place only in the South, resulting in the formation of the Republic of Korea, led by American-educated Syngman Rhee. The Soviets not only rejected this government but set up a rival government in the North—the Democratic People's Republic of Korea—led by Communist Kim Il Sung.

President Truman was in an extremely difficult situation, but was determined to continue his policy of containing and preventing the spread of Communism. However, before any plans could be put into place, the North Korean People's Army marched into the South and lit the fuse on another war.

THE INVASION OF SOUTH KOREA
June 1950

After a period of escalating border conflicts, units of the North Korean People's Army stormed across the thirty-eighth parallel on June 27, 1950, and quickly occupied the South Korean capital of Seoul. The ideological conflict between the Communist North and the non-Communist South had suddenly turned highly volatile. Although wary of inciting all-out war, President Truman ordered American air and sea forces to support South Korea, and the United Nations called upon the assistance of member states.

The North Koreans advanced swiftly, and it was not long until South Korean forces and the US Eighth Army had been pushed back into the southeastern corner of the Korean Peninsula, near the city of Pusan. American forces under the command of General Douglas MacArthur managed to stabilize and hold a line along the Nakdong River, north of Pusan, which became known as the Pusan Perimeter.

With the situation becoming increasingly desperate, MacArthur directed troops in a risky amphibious assault on Inchon, near Seoul. The attack was a major success: Seoul was retaken and Communist troops were driven back north of the thirty-eighth parallel.

A Communist alliance between China and the Soviet Union in defense of North Korea was inevitable. Nonetheless, General MacArthur led the US Army on a swift and successful Northern invasion on September 27, 1950, and North Korean troops were driven back to the Chinese border at the Yalu River.

THE KOREAN WAR: STALEMATE
1953

On October 8, 1950, with the North Korean Army driven up toward the Chinese border, China's military and political leader, Chairman Mao Zedong, assembled the Chinese People's Volunteer Army to join with North Korea in a counterattack.

The might of the Communist alliance overwhelmed UN forces, and by mid-December they had been driven back to the thirty-eighth parallel, where they struggled to maintain a defensive line. The relentless Chinese offensive saw UN forces outnumbered; following a series of night attacks, Seoul was recaptured by Communist forces on January 4, 1951. The situation was grim and the loss of life escalating. In retaliation, General MacArthur ordered a gradual advance northward, in what became known as the "meatgrinder." After inflicting heavy casualties on Communist troops, America regained control of the ruined city of Seoul by mid-March 1951.

MacArthur began to lobby for an expansion of the war into China, even suggesting that nuclear weapons be used. President Truman, fearing the conflict could explode into a third world war, vetoed the invasion of China and fired MacArthur for insubordination.

Heavy fighting continued, mostly along the thirty-eighth parallel, but the conflict had reached stalemate. Peace talks began at the end of June 1951, but it was not until April 1953 that a ceasefire was agreed. By the time the armistice was signed on July 27, 1953, around 3 million troops and civilians had been killed in the Korean War, yet the border between North and South Korea remained essentially unchanged.

DWIGHT D. EISENHOWER
October 14, 1890–March 28, 1969

Dwight David "Ike" Eisenhower was born into a Texas farming family. After graduating from West Point Military Academy in 1915, he launched himself into a prestigious military career that culminated in his appointment as Supreme Commander of the Allied Forces in Europe during World War Two, leading the invasions of Sicily and Italy, as well as Operation Overlord.

Having demonstrated his leadership ability, Eisenhower was persuaded by the Republican Party to run for president in 1952. Campaigning under the slogan "I like Ike" and a promise to end the Korean War, Eisenhower triumphed over Democrat Adlai Stevenson, and entered the White House at age sixty-two.

Eisenhower's presidency was dominated by the Cold War. After securing a truce in Korea, he promoted the use of covert action, using the CIA and U-2 spy planes to gather intelligence on Communist activities. He increased American involvement in Southeast Asia and sent the first American troops to Vietnam in 1955. In 1957, he created the Eisenhower Doctrine, which proclaimed America's right to aid any country threatened by Communist hostility. During his time in office, the United States became the world's foremost nuclear power.

On the domestic front, Eisenhower signed into law the Civil Rights Acts of 1957 and 1961, implemented the integration of American military forces, and sent federal troops into Little Rock, Arkansas, to enforce the desegregation of local schools. He also supported and authorized the construction of the Interstate Highway System.

Eisenhower retired to his farm in Pennsylvania in 1961, after two terms in office. He died in Washington, D.C., eight years later.

THE CIVIL RIGHTS MOVEMENT: THE ORIGINS
1909–48

Despite the abolition of slavery in 1865, millions of white Americans, particularly in the South, remained opposed to racial integration—let alone equality—and African Americans were still marginalized by a series of local customs and "Jim Crow" laws designed to segregate the races.

Segregation did not simply mean the use of separate facilities: In every aspect of public life, African Americans were forced to use vastly inferior amenities, from schools and parks to transportation and restaurants. Meanwhile, the armed forces and civil service were segregated, and legal loopholes allowed individual states to disenfranchise their African American citizens.

Following the establishment of the NAACP in 1909, segregation was gradually challenged in the courts. But it took two world wars and the deaths of thousands of black Americans in defense of their country for the government to begin passing integration legislation. On July 26, 1948, President Truman signed Executive Order 9981, which decreed: "There shall be equality of treatment and opportunity to all persons in the Armed services without regard to race."

The desegregation of the armed forces did little to change life for the ordinary African American, but by the mid-twentieth century, the mood was beginning to shift. When migration from the rural South to the industrialized North increased after World War Two, African American communities found strength in numbers. Crucially, millions of black voters began to vote for politicians sympathetic to their cause, and the Civil Rights Movement quickly gained momentum.

THE CIVIL RIGHTS MOVEMENT: *BROWN V. BOARD OF EDUCATION* 1954

Although slow progress was being made in the field of civil rights, segregation was still enforceable by law in the South in the early 1950s, sanctioned by the "separate but equal" precedent of the *Plessy v. Ferguson* ruling of 1896. Nowhere was this doctrine shown to be more meaningless than in the public school system, where the inequality between schools for white children and schools for black children could not have been more apparent.

In 1951, Linda Brown, an African American girl from Topeka, Kansas, was refused admission to the local white elementary school, even though the nearest segregated school was much farther away. Sponsored by the NAACP, a group of Topeka parents led by Linda's father, Oliver Brown, sought an injunction on segregation in Topeka public schools.

The case was heard in the Kansas District Court in June 1951, with the NAACP arguing that the "separate but equal" doctrine fostered inequality by treating African American students as inferior. The Board of Education counterargued that segregated schools prepared African American students for a future in which they would experience segregation daily.

The District Court cited *Plessy v. Ferguson* and found in favor of the Board of Education, but the NAACP appealed to the Supreme Court, using *Brown* as an umbrella for five near-identical cases from different states. On May 17, 1954, the Supreme Court ruled that separate school facilities were inherently unequal; in a huge boost for the Civil Rights Movement, segregation in American schools became illegal.

THE CIVIL RIGHTS MOVEMENT: ROSA PARKS
1955

On December 1, 1955, Rosa Parks, an African American seamstress, refused to give up her seat to a white man on a bus in Montgomery, Alabama, and was arrested for defying segregation laws.

As the secretary of her local NAACP chapter, Parks volunteered to act as a legal test case against the Montgomery authorities and the laws of segregation. The African American community of Montgomery turned to Martin Luther King, Jr., the inspirational young pastor of the local Baptist church, to help organize a protest. Together with other community leaders, King circulated thousands of handbills calling for all African Americans to boycott the city's buses on the day of Rosa Parks's trial.

On December 5, 1955, around 90 percent of Montgomery's African American bus passengers joined the protest, and the Montgomery Improvement Association (MIA) was established that very evening, with King as its president. For over a year, the MIA guided the protest, and an estimated 17,000 African Americans walked, cycled, or used organized carpool facilities.

The Montgomery Bus Company was losing revenue quickly, and the protest fanned the flames of racial tension. But despite a campaign of harassment that included conspiracy charges against members of the MIA, bombings, arson, and unlawful arrests, the boycott continued. On November 13, 1956, the Supreme Court ruled that segregation on public transportation was unconstitutional.

MARTIN LUTHER KING, JR.
January 15, 1929–April 4, 1968

Martin Luther King, Jr., was born in Georgia, the son and grandson of local pastors. Educated at segregated public schools until the age of fifteen, he received a BA from the traditionally black Morehouse College, a Bachelor of Divinity from Crozer Theological Seminary in Pennsylvania, and a Ph.D. from Boston University.

In 1954, King became pastor of the Dexter Avenue Baptist Church in Montgomery, Alabama. As an active civil rights campaigner and member of the NAACP, he was thrust into the national spotlight when he led the 1955 Montgomery Bus Boycott. He emerged from the protest a proven community leader and was elected president of the Southern Christian Leadership Conference in 1957. Motivated by the teachings of India's Mahatma Gandhi, King's legacy to the Conference was the notion of nonviolent civil disobedience.

Over the next decade, King and the SCLC led a number of high-profile protests across the United States, including the Birmingham campaign of 1963, in which protesters boycotted segregationist businesses and purposely filled the city jails in order to force the authorities to negotiate. In August 1963, King led 250,000 people in a peaceful march on Washington, where he delivered his world-famous "I have a dream" speech, invoking a nation in which people would "not be judged by the color of their skin, but by the content of their character." He was awarded the Nobel Peace Prize in 1964.

King's campaigns were both inspirational and controversial, and he garnered many enemies. On April 4, 1968, he was assassinated in Memphis, Tennessee, by escaped convict James Earl Ray.

THE ELECTION OF JOHN F. KENNEDY
1960

John Fitzgerald Kennedy—JFK—was born into a privileged and powerful Irish-American family from Massachusetts. His father, Joseph, was one of the nation's richest men and a former member of Franklin D. Roosevelt's cabinet. After serving in the US Navy during World War Two, Kennedy joined the Democratic Party and embarked upon a political career that had been choreographed by his well-connected father.

In 1958, having been elected to the Senate for a second term, JFK set his sights on the presidency. The odds were against him: at forty-one, he was very young, and as a practicing Roman Catholic, he faced opposition from Southern Protestants. Nonetheless, he was victorious in the primaries, defeating Senator Lyndon B. Johnson to become the Democratic nominee in 1960. He was outspoken against Communism and advocated a "New Frontier" of domestic and foreign reform that ranged from international aid to the space program.

For the first time, image played a central role in a presidential election. The first ever televised presidential debate, between Kennedy and his Republican opponent Richard Nixon, attracted over 70 million viewers. While Nixon did well with radio listeners, he was less impressive to the television audience: He looked tired, sported a five o'clock shadow, and was no match for Kennedy's photogenic vitality.

Kennedy won the election, one of the closest-run in American history, and used his inaugural address to call for a change in domestic policy: "Ask not what your country can do for you; ask what you can do for your country."

THE BAY OF PIGS INVASION
April 1961

Kennedy began his presidency with high hopes for a new era of American-Soviet cooperation alongside new Soviet leader Nikita Khrushchev. Before long, however, his optimism gave way to the ongoing tensions of the Cold War.

Cuba was a particularly pressing concern. In 1959, Fidel Castro's Communist Party had claimed Cuba, creating a Communist stronghold within easy reach of the United States. Under President Eisenhower, the CIA had begun plans for an invasion of Cuba. They intended to equip Cuban exiles rather than use American personnel, and to drop them onto Cuba's Bay of Pigs in the hope that they would incite an anti-Castro revolt. Once in office, Kennedy gave the CIA his approval for the invasion.

The three-day invasion in April 1961 proved a disaster. A preemptive air strike was not as damaging as was intended, and succeeded only in putting Castro on the alert. Furthermore, the invasion forces were poorly equipped, ill informed, and not backed up by a credible contingency plan. Wary of international criticism or Soviet retaliation, Kennedy canceled a number of air attacks and ordered the US Navy, poised off the coast of Cuba, not to take action. Meanwhile, the CIA had underestimated Castro's popularity in Cuba, rendering the proposed counterrevolution almost impossible.

The Cuban rebels, let down by the CIA and by the US Armed Forces, were mostly either killed or captured. The Bay of Pigs invasion was a dismal failure that arguably served to increase pro-Communist sentiment in Cuba.

THE CUBAN MISSILE CRISIS
October 1962

Following the attempted invasion of Cuba by American-backed forces, the Cuban Communists turned to the Soviet Union for support. With the Cold War at its height, and encouraged by what he saw as a chaotic and inept attack at the Bay of Pigs, Soviet Premier Khrushchev was eager to strengthen military ties with Cuba, whose proximity to the United States mainland made for an ideal Communist missile base.

On October 14, 1962, American intelligence detected Soviet missile bases under construction in Cuba. This time, Kennedy took decisive action. Unwilling to risk all-out war, he stopped short of approving air attacks on Soviet bases in Cuba, but ordered a naval blockade and demanded that Soviet arms and bases be removed. As a backup, he put the army on full alert for an invasion of Cuba.

Khrushchev announced that the Soviet Union would ignore the blockade and Kennedy's ultimatum, and Soviet battleships advanced on Cuba. The standoff intensified into talk of nuclear warfare and Mutually Assured Destruction, with Kennedy stating that the United States would "regard any nuclear missile launched from Cuba against any nation in the Western Hemisphere as an attack on the United States, requiring a full retaliatory response upon the Soviet Union."

The crisis lasted thirteen days, after which Kennedy and Khrushchev agreed on a resolution: The Soviet Union would dismantle its bases in Cuba, while the United States would respect Cuban sovereignty and remove American missiles from Turkey. Kennedy's tough stance seemed at last to have laid the Bay of Pigs debacle to rest.

THE ASSASSINATION OF JFK
November 22, 1963

On November 22, 1963, President Kennedy and First Lady Jacqueline Kennedy were making a tour of Dallas, Texas, on the campaign trail. As the presidential motorcade turned in front of the Texas School Book Depository, two bullets struck the president in the head and neck. He died half an hour later.

Within hours, twenty-four-year-old Texan Lee Harvey Oswald was arrested. Two days later, as television crews filmed Oswald being transported to a secure jail, Dallas strip-club owner Jack Ruby pushed through a crowd of police officers and shot him dead.

The nation's grief and shock was immense—hundreds of thousands of mourners later paid their respects as Kennedy lay in state at the White House—and immediately fueled conspiracy theories. Vice President Lyndon B. Johnson was sworn in hours after the assassination and instantly called for an investigation, headed by Chief Justice Earl Warren. After ten months, and more than 500 witness statements, the Warren Commission concluded that both Lee Harvey Oswald and Jack Ruby had acted entirely alone.

Criticism of the Warren Commission was widespread, and its findings did little to quash conspiracy theories. In 1976, a House of Representatives Select Committee on Assassinations relaunched the inquiry, producing a series of revelations about the CIA and the FBI during the Kennedy administration. The Committee concluded that Kennedy "was probably assassinated as a result of a conspiracy."

Unsolved to this day, the Kennedy assassination remains one of the most widely debated events in modern American history.

LYNDON B. JOHNSON
August 27, 1908–January 22, 1973

Lyndon Baines Johnson came from humble roots in Texas. He worked his way through school and earned his own tuition at Southwest Texas Teachers' College. His experiences teaching some of the country's poorest children later influenced his domestic policy.

Johnson's father had served on the Texas legislature and used his influence to get Johnson hired as secretary to a Democratic Congressman in 1931. He became head of Texas's National Youth Administration in 1935, won a seat in the House of Representatives in 1937, and was elected to the Senate in 1948. Johnson was a skilled politician, a master of negotiation, and a great admirer of Franklin D. Roosevelt and the New Deal. He ran against John F. Kennedy for the 1960 presidential nomination, but was eventually chosen as Kennedy's running mate, possibly for his Southern support network.

Less than two hours after the assassination of President Kennedy, Vice President Johnson took the oath of office aboard Air Force One. His first public address was an emotional appeal reflecting the nation's grief: "An assassin's bullet has thrust upon me the awesome burden of the presidency. I am here to say that I need the help of all Americans, in all of America."

Johnson believed that the government should be obligated to serve the disadvantaged, a stance he put into practice through his passionate promotion of a "Great Society" in which education, federal aid, urban renewal, and civil rights were championed. His popularity was adversely affected, however, by a period of increased military activity in Vietnam.

Johnson retired to Texas in 1969, and died there in 1973.

THE GREAT SOCIETY AND THE CIVIL RIGHTS ACT
1964–65

The spirit of Roosevelt's New Deal and the ambition of Kennedy's New Frontier lay at the heart of Johnson's program of domestic reform, outlined six months before his landslide reelection in 1964. The substance of "The Great Society"—"abundance and liberty for all" and "an end to poverty and racial injustice"—was laid out in a range of impressive legislation, with task forces assigned to fourteen areas of society, from agriculture to inner-city housing. A series of acts established scholarships and student loans, and pumped billions of dollars into public schools, while the Medicare and Medicaid programs provided federal medical insurance for the elderly and the poor.

Perhaps the greatest advances were in civil rights, a focal point of Johnson's presidency from the outset. But although 1964's Civil Rights Act outlawed gender, religious, or racial discrimination, it had many opponents in the South; its failure to address the problem of voter qualification meant that literacy tests and other local legislation designed to disenfranchise African Americans remained in place.

The Civil Rights Movement fought for a legislative solution, organizing protests throughout 1964's "Freedom Summer," during which passions often overflowed. Three white activists were murdered in Philadelphia, Mississippi, while police wielding cattle prods confronted peaceful protesters in Selma, Alabama, in January 1965.

Following Johnson's passionate address to Congress, his Voting Rights Act was passed in August 1965, outlawing any legislation designed to restrict access to the vote. However, the acute economic divide between black and white citizens meant there was still work to be done, signaling a significant shift in the Civil Rights Movement.

MALCOLM X AND
THE RISE OF BLACK POWER

M alcolm Little was born in Nebraska on May 19, 1925. He
escaped a fire at age four and his father was killed two years
later; both traumatic incidents were believed to be racially motivated.
Little dropped out of school and became involved in crime.

It was in prison that Little learned about the Nation of Islam, a
religious movement also known as the Black Muslims. He dropped his
surname in favor of "Malcolm X," and became an outspoken radical
leader, distancing himself from Martin Luther King, Jr. "I don't see
any American dream," he said, "I see an American nightmare."

In 1964, Malcolm X broke with the Nation of Islam and
began preaching a broader vision of racial harmony that embraced
international human rights. A year later, on February 21, he was
assassinated—purportedly for his "treachery"—by members of the
Black Muslim movement. His shift in focus prior to his death went
largely unheeded by a generation of young activists, disillusioned by
the impact of the nonviolent movement and already stirred by his
one-time hard-line rhetoric. Posthumously, Malcolm X inspired a
radicalization of the Civil Rights Movement, which became known
as "Black Power."

The Black Panthers were one facet of the movement's new
direction. Established in Oakland, California, in 1966 with the
original aim of protecting African Americans against police brutality,
the Black Panthers soon expanded into cities nationwide, attracting
a varied membership and a great deal of police suspicion. Violent
confrontations with police became commonplace and ultimately
overshadowed the organization's many commendable socialist ideals,
and the Black Panthers disbanded by the mid-1970s.

THE VIETNAM
WAR YEARS

THE GULF OF TONKIN RESOLUTION
1964

When China became a Communist nation in 1949, the United States adopted a policy of "containment" in an attempt to prevent the spread of Communism in Southeast Asia. The primary source of concern was Vietnam, which had been partitioned by the Geneva Treaty of 1954 into Communist North and anti-Communist South Vietnam, with the stipulation that a democratic election should be held in 1956 to reunite the country. The election never took place: The Eisenhower administration, fearing a Communist win, instead financed a pro-US government in Saigon, South Vietnam.

President Kennedy dramatically increased the number of American "military advisers" in the region from 700 to 15,000. Their task was to provide commando training for the South Vietnamese forces. Just weeks before Kennedy's assassination, the CIA helped engineer a military coup that overthrew the prime minister of South Vietnam, Ngo Dinh Diem, who was losing control to the Communist North Vietnamese forces.

In 1964, President Johnson expressed reservations about military action in Vietnam, but he knew the spread of Communism in Southeast Asia could lose him the presidency. In August 1964, an American spy ship claimed to have been pursued and attacked by a North Vietnamese patrol boat in the Gulf of Tonkin. The attack, though never confirmed, was the "Pearl Harbor" opportunity Johnson needed. He ordered an immediate air strike on North Vietnam and reported the Gulf of Tonkin encounter to Congress. The resultant Gulf of Tonkin Resolution amounted to a declaration of war, giving Johnson carte blanche to take "all necessary measures to repel armed attack" in Vietnam.

THE VIETNAM WAR
1965–73

In February 1965, six months after the Gulf of Tonkin Resolution, the Communist forces attacked an American air base in South Vietnam. President Johnson retaliated with a series of air strikes, 200,000 American ground troops, and a sustained bombing campaign. By the end of the year, South Korea, Australia, New Zealand, Thailand, and the Philippines had entered the war.

Over the next two years, the war grew ever more brutal. The highly toxic defoliant Agent Orange was dropped across Vietnam to deprive the Viet Cong of their forest cover, "search and destroy" missions killed civilians as well as the enemy, and the body count soared. The Tet Offensive, launched by the Viet Cong across South Vietnam in January 1968 ("Tet" being the lunar New Year), made it clear that American victory was far from imminent. With over half a million American troops active in Vietnam, opinion began to swing into the antiwar camp.

In March 1968, Johnson called for renewed peace negotiations and a halt to bombing raids, and unveiled plans for the withdrawal of American troops. The peace talks reached stalemate, however, and it was not until 1973—over two decades after the United States began its involvement in Vietnamese politics—that peace was brokered under President Nixon.

This settlement was a compromise that failed to resolve the North-South divide. Two years later, South Vietnam fell to the Communist North. Having spent $100 billion, lost 58,000 troops, and dropped 7 million tons of bombs during the conflict, the United States did not intervene when Vietnam finally united under Communist leadership.

COUNTERCULTURE, CONTROVERSY, AND A GIANT LEAP FOR MANKIND
1960–73

The 1960s heralded a period of cultural rebellion. A new "counterculture" undermined traditional values, embraced liberal expression through music and fashion, and championed human rights from Black Power to spiritual freedom. While psychologist Timothy Leary encouraged a generation to "turn on, tune in, drop out" with LSD, the first widely available contraceptive pill gave way to a sexual revolution—"free love"—and advanced the feminist movement.

By 1970, an increasing number of women wanted the right to secure a legal abortion written into the Constitution. In March of that year, Norma McCorvey—known in court as "Jane Roe"—brought a suit before Dallas County District Attorney Henry Wade, on the grounds that Texas had denied her her constitutional right to an abortion. *Roe v. Wade* went all the way to the Supreme Court, which, in January 1973, ruled that the prohibition of abortion was unconstitutional, overturning the abortion laws of forty-six states.

Meanwhile, the United States and the Soviet Union were battling for cosmic supremacy. The Soviet Union had launched the world's first satellite and a canine cosmonaut in 1957, and upped the stakes in May 1961 by sending the first man into space. Refusing to be outdone, and with a manned moon landing as their ultimate goal, Presidents Kennedy and Nixon prioritized the Space Race throughout the 1960s. Finally, on July 20, 1969, the world watched in awe as Neil Armstrong stepped onto the moon, uttering the immortal words: "That's one small step for [a] man, one giant leap for mankind."

RICHARD NIXON
January 9, 1913–April 22, 1994

Richard Nixon was born to Quaker parents in California. The family suffered financially during the 1920s and Nixon attended modest schools, although he was an ambitious student. He studied law at Duke University, in North Carolina, and became a successful lawyer.

After serving in the US Navy during World War Two, Nixon ran for Congress in California, as a Republican. His tactics during these 1946 elections—tapping into Cold War paranoia—set the pattern for successive campaigns.

In the House of Representatives, Nixon built on his trademark anti-Communist stance by relentlessly pursuing the case of Alger Hiss, who had served under the Roosevelt administration but subsequently been accused of Soviet espionage. Hiss's conviction helped carry Nixon into the Senate in 1950. He stood as Eisenhower's running mate in 1952, but stumbled when allegations about illegal donations to his campaign appeared. Nixon's response, a televised financial disclosure during which he even disclosed the gift of his puppy, was dismissed as mawkish, but paid off at the polls.

Nixon was a dynamic vice president, undertaking a number of high-profile diplomatic visits. In 1960, he was the clear choice for the presidential nomination, but when he lost to John F. Kennedy and later failed to win Governor of California, his political days seemed numbered. His remarkable comeback to win the presidency in 1968 was heralded as a political revival, but his achievements in the Oval Office were overshadowed by scandal, resulting in his resignation.

Nixon retired to New Jersey and gradually regained international respect as an elder statesman. He died in New York, at age eighty-one.

CAMBODIA
1969–70

In public, President Nixon's primary concern was the replacement of American troops in Vietnam with Vietnamese troops, a process termed "Vietnamization." In private, Nixon and his national security adviser (later secretary of state) Henry Kissinger had a new concern: Cambodia, west of Vietnam, had been providing military support to North Vietnamese troops in South Vietnam. The possible spread of Communism to Cambodia was intolerable to Nixon, who sanctioned undisclosed bombing raids on Communist bases in March 1969. In effect, Nixon and Kissinger embarked upon a secret war.

The bombings continued throughout the year, concealed from the American public, who believed their president was scaling back the war in Southeast Asia. Then, in April 1970, Nixon appeared on national television, fluffing his lines and pointing to a rudimentary map of Cambodia, announcing that American troops were in the process of invading the country in order to wipe out its Communist bases. He failed to say that America was already a year into its campaign in Cambodia.

This was not the de-escalation Nixon had promised, and the press largely reflected the nation's dismay. Antiwar protests picked up, and in some cases became violent. At Kent State University in Ohio, four students died after National Guardsmen opened fire on demonstrators; two more were killed at Jackson State College in Mississippi days later.

United States action destabilized the Cambodian government, facilitating the rise of the Khmer Rouge, a Communist movement that terrorized Cambodians for much of the decade. At home, Nixon's sanctioning of secret bombing raids would soon form part of his public disgrace.

WATERGATE AND NIXON'S RESIGNATION
1972–74

On June 17, 1972, there was a break-in at the Democratic Party's headquarters in Washington's Watergate complex. The five men arrested at the scene were linked to Nixon's Committee to Re-elect the President (known later as CREEP), and two further committee members were arrested soon after. The burglary was covered in the press, but nothing in these reports suggested presidential involvement, and Nixon was reelected in a landslide.

Rumors of high-level corruption began when it emerged that the detainees included a former FBI agent, a former CIA agent, and four Cubans, three of whom had been involved in the Bay of Pigs debacle. The *Washington Post* published a series of stories provided by secret informant "Deep Throat," claiming that the burglary had been carried out on White House orders and subsequently covered up.

The Senate appointed a Select Committee to investigate the Watergate scandal, which uncovered a tangled web of break-ins, campaign sabotage, and illicit surveillance emanating from within the White House. President Nixon made feeble efforts to distance himself from the scandal, but the case against him gathered strength when he refused to hand over taped recordings of Oval Office conversations. When the tapes were finally subpoenaed in July 1974, Nixon was clearly implicated in an authorized cover-up.

The House of Representatives began impeachment proceedings, charging the president with a list of "high crimes and misdemeanors." On August 8, 1974, Nixon announced his resignation. He was later "rehabilitated" into the Republican Party after President Gerald Ford granted him "a full, free, and absolute pardon."

INDEX